West Africa

VOLUME TWO

VOLUME ONE

BEFORE 1800

Revised Edition
Seventh Printing

'..brings home the continuity of
African history and culture'
—*Teacher Education*

West Africa in History

BY W. F. CONTON
B.A.

Chief Education Officer, Sierra Leone
Sometime Headmaster, Accra High School, Ghana

VOLUME TWO

Since 1800

DEDICATED
TO MY CHILDREN

FIRST PUBLISHED IN 1963
SECOND IMPRESSION 1964
THIRD IMPRESSION 1965
REVISED NEW EDITION, FOURTH IMPRESSION 1966
FIFTH IMPRESSION 1966

This book is copyright under the Berne Convention. Apart from any fair dealing for the purpose of private study, research, criticism or review, as permitted under the Copyright Act 1956, no portion may be reproduced by any process without written permission. Enquiry should be made to the author or his heirs

© William Conton

Second Edition © William Conton

INTRODUCTION

This volume completes the author's 1000-year odyssey around the vast West African landscape, bringing us up to date with events to 1966, when the book was last revised. Up and down the mighty rivers, across the vast desert, through the dense jungles and along the unending coastline, all of which predestined the history; and throughout the relentless technological innovation, the spread of iron, the advance of the sailing ship, the power of steam, all of which tamed the geography, it has been a fascinating journey, with twists and turns, peaks and troughs. Volume 2 (Since 1800) necessarily approaches its material from a different angle, that of the modern nation state rather than the tribe. My late father remains the dedicated Africanist throughout the entire colonial interregnum (and over the ten years or so he must have spent researching and writing these two volumes), every now and then implicitly chiding the occupiers and applauding the struggles of the oppressed West Africans. And then, after Independence is finally attained in the late-fifties and early-sixties, he manfully records without comment the debacles of the mid-sixties. A final lesson of history perhaps for the author and his readers. One wishes the story could continue to the present day and even beyond. How will it all end?

Paul Conton
Freetown, August, 2022

PREFACE TO REVISED EDITION

Volume Two follows a pattern similar to Volume One. The time chart at the end is intended not to be memorized, but to be completed. Teacher and pupil are provided thereby with an opportunity to make use of a device illustrating relationships in time through relationships in space: for that is what a time chart does. The most important events in the known history of the four separate areas of West Africa have already been inserted. You can see which years are omitted, and these omissions often mean gaps in our knowledge. With the help of some of the publications mentioned in Volume One, and under the guidance of the teacher, the pupil can fill these gaps as more knowledge of West Africa's past becomes available, and can compile, for one or more of the four areas, a fuller time chart of his own in his exercise book. He can also trace, even in the incomplete chart now provided, the comparative progress made by the four areas in the social, economic and constitutional fields over any period. But pupils and teachers are asked to regard the chart as a supplement to the text, not as a substitute for it; for otherwise false conclusions are certain to be drawn. And the addition of other related events elsewhere has deliberately been left as a project for each class.

I have used the word 'civilized' several times in the text. To me it simply means 'having achieved mastery over the forces of nature and the instincts of man'. It does *not* necessarily mean '*Western* civilization'. Its opposite is 'primitive'.

I have throughout spelled the name Ibo in this form. It is also spelled Igbo and the West African Examinations Council uses the form Igbo in its examination on the language. Pupils should be familiar with both spellings.

Volumes One and Two together of this textbook cover the School Certificate/G.C.E. syllabus for the History of West Africa, A.D. 1000 to the Present Day. This second volume on its own may also be found a useful textbook for the alternative paper, the History of Africa in the Nineteenth and Twentieth Centuries.

CONTENTS

Introduction...Paul Conton

The Nineteenth Century: The Gambia, Sierra Leone and the Gold Coast 11

Nigeria in the Nineteenth Century 35

Sovereignty Regained: The Gambia, Sierra Leone, Ghana 57

Nigeria: from Unification toFederation 71

Nationalism in French-speakingWest Africa and the Movement towards African Unity 89

Liberia 103

Independent West Africa: The Commonwealth Countries 111

Independent West Africa: The French-speaking Countries .. 127

MAPS

GHANA TODAY 25

THE YORUBA EMPIRE 36

THE EAST AND THE DELTA 47

THE FULANI EMPIRE 52

SIERRA LEONE 61

THE FEDERATION OF NIGERIA IN 1965 72

AFRICA TODAY 90

LIBERIA 104

1
The Nineteenth Century: The Gambia, Sierra Leone and the Gold Coast

a. THE GAMBIA

The French wars and the ban on slave trading

In 1785 the British Crown returned to the Company of Merchants trading to Africa the Gambia forts which, as bastions of the Province of Senegambia, had been administered by the Crown for twenty years. Few people at that time foresaw that the Crown would shortly be persuaded to resume responsibility not only for those forts, but for all other forts and factories occupied by the British in Sierra Leone, the Gambia and the Gold Coast. Yet this is precisely what happened in 1808, 1816 and 1821.

The two main reasons for this unexpected development were the effects on the Company's trade of the war between Britain and France (amongst others) which lasted from 1793 to 1815, and of the ban on slave trading which came into effect in Denmark in 1804, Britain in 1807, the U.S. in 1808, Sweden in 1813, Holland in 1814, France in 1815, Spain in 1816 and Portugal in 1817. The war affected the volume of trade; the gradual progress towards the abolition of the transatlantic slave trade affected the character of trade. Since this company was organized especially for slave trading, both affected its profits.

However, these effects were felt only gradually. It is true that the French had been very quick off the mark in their successful assault on Freetown in 1794; but the Company no doubt hoped that the subsequent British control of the seas and the fact that Britain had finally won the war would enable it to make good some of its losses. And the ban on the slave trade was evaded at first much more often than observed. The kings did not like the slavers. In 1816 the King of Kombo only ceded Banjol Island (the modern St Mary's) to Governor MacCarthy's envoy Captain Alexander Grant because six weeks before the Spanish had abducted twenty of his relatives, and he was looking for a protector. But there were all too many Africans who had formed the habit of supplying the now illegal slave trade with fellow Africans, and who still sought the profits which this practice brought, in spite of the watchfulness of the British and other European navies.

The development of Bathurst

The peace treaty of 1814 returned Albreda to the French and the Portendic gum trade to the British, both having changed hands during the war. That year also saw the placing of the Company's forts in Gambia and Sierra Leone in the charge of an army officer named Charles MacCarthy, who became Governor of them all in 1816. He now had the small town which was forming on St Mary's Island named 'Bathurst' after Earl Bathurst, the British Secretary of State, and garrisoned it with eighty soldiers. James Island now ceased to be the headquarters of the British in the Gambia, and was replaced by Bathurst, mainly because the King of Barra, within whose territory James Island lay, was proving much more hostile to the British than the King of Kombo, who owned St Mary's. Everything was done to encourage the development of Bathurst. The hostility of the King of Barra, who at this time was Kollimanka Mane, was overcome sufficiently to get him to allow the removal of building stones from Dog Island for use in Bathurst. The traders of Goree and St Louis were offered free land in Bathurst on condition that they built houses that would last for a reasonable time; and so many of them accepted the offer that Goree was abandoned to the French. The population of Bathurst rose from 100 in 1817 to 1,800 in 1826.

The transatlantic slave trade, now forbidden to British and French alike, was not stamped out until 1864. The British Navy took any slave ships it was able to catch to Sierra Leone, where an Admiralty court dealt with the slavers and released their victims, who joined the ranks of the 'liberated Africans', as you will remember the fourth group of settlers in Freetown was called. The French were either less vigilant or less willing to enforce the ban: until about 1831 slaves were still going over-land from Albreda to Goree, and from there were being shipped overseas along the same route as before the ban. Some ex-slaves who had learnt how to build houses and lay out streets in Freetown were brought to Bathurst to undertake similar work. Also from Freetown, and much less welcome, came a number of expelled criminals. Fugitives from slavery and imprisonment in Senegal also made their way to Bathurst.

Economic development

The colony developed slowly and, as in all British colonies, this development was in two main directions — as a producer of raw material for British industry, and as a market for the finished products of the same industry. The economy of West Africa was to serve the economy of Britain just as slavishly after as before the banning of the Atlantic slave trade. But the emphasis of the British economy had been changed during the eighteenth century; as she developed her industries she required more and more raw materials for them, and more imports of agricultural products to feed her growing population. Consequently, vegetable oils, beeswax, hides and gum, all bound for Britain, replaced slaves bound for the plantations of the New World on the ships leaving the Gambia during the

The Nineteenth Century: Gambia, Sierra Leone and the Gold Coast

nineteenth century. In 1817 nine-tenths by value of exports from the Gambia consisted of beeswax. In 1822 timber for building and furniture (as distinct from wood for dyeing) was first exported, and in 1830 so were groundnuts, which in 1848 had easily overtaken beeswax and made up two-thirds of the value of the exports from the territory. Forty acres of groundnuts were under cultivation on St Mary's Island alone by 1844.

The Gambia becomes a colony

The British could shape the economy but not the climate of the Gambia, nor even ward off the effects of the climate. The mortality rate amongst the British soldiers and traders here was terrifying. It was much less so if they slept in ships on the river itself than if they slept ashore; which perhaps suggests that malaria, carried by mosquitoes breeding in stagnant water, was the biggest killer. In four months during the 1825 rainy season eighty-seven of the 108 British troops billeted ashore died, but not one of the ninety-one billeted on board the transport *Surrey*. Incredibly, these ninety-one were then given the vacant accommodation ashore, and seventy-three of them died before the end of the year. Between 1816 and 1827, 276 of the 399 men of the Royal African Corps sent to the Gambia died in Bathurst, and African and West Indian troops, ex-slaves from Sierra Leone, had to be used in this garrison from now on.

The reason for the presence of this corps here was that although the British Crown did not take over the administration of the colony until 1821, from 1816 to 1818 Gambia was technically a military post under a commandant responsible to the Governor of Sierra Leone. In 1818 a civil government was set up by the Governor, with courts, a legislature, a garrison and a mayor of Bathurst, all still subject ultimately to the Governor of Sierra Leone. It was a short step from this to the passing in 1821 of the Act of the British Parliament which formally transferred all the legal rights of the Company of Merchants in the Gambia and the Gold Coast to the British Crown, represented by the Governor of Sierra Leone. A Lieutenant-Governor in Bathurst acted for the Governor. Laws were to be made in Sierra Leone for the Gambia.

Almost immediately there arose in the Gambia a demand for administrative independence from Sierra Leone. In 1827 the Gambia commandant was allowed to correspond direct with London, and two years later the Lieutenant-Governor was given a similar right. Both legislatively and financially, however, Gambia remained dependent on Sierra Leone, having in 1826 to borrow £1,000 from Sierra Leone.

The coming of missionaries

The first missionaries arrived in Bathurst in the same year as Crown Colony status — 1821. The first of these were members of the Society of Friends, and Methodists and an Anglican chaplain to the forces followed soon after. They opened schools for girls that year, and for boys the following year. In 1823 the

West Africa in History

French Sisters of Charity started work in Bathurst, in 1834 the Wesleyan church, which still stands today, was opened with 250 members, and in 1849 three sisters arrived from the Convent of St Joseph at Cluny, and later became nurses in the civilian hospital opened in 1854. Like the troops, many of these missionaries soon fell victims to ill health. The Diocese of Sierra Leone, created in 1852, included the Gambia, and in 1855 the West Indian Mission to West Africa began to work in the Gambia and Guinea.

Neighbours of the Gambia

We must never forget that the history of European contact with West Africa is only part of the history of West Africa, and we must now look at the peoples with whom the European administrators, soldiers and missionaries were coming into increasing contact.

Occupying in this century both banks of the river were the Mandingo, originally citizens of that empire of Mali which we studied in Volume One. Their main home now was a region 700 miles east of Bathurst. Then there were the Joloff, whose kingdom of Bur Salum extended 100 miles inland from the Atlantic, to the north of the Gambia. They had moved down from the east to reach the coast somewhere between the Senegal and the Gambia.

The Fula we met earlier, and know that although they were later arrivals than the Mandingo and Joloff, they had by the mid-nineteenth century already been present for some 350 years at least in the region where the Senegal and Gambia rise. Whilst their urbanized brothers in Northern Nigeria were conducting their Jihad or holy war at the beginning of this century, the more peaceful and still pagan Fula in Senegambia were mainly tending their herds.

Then there were the Jola, the people with the longest history of settlement in the Gambia. Most Jola are, like the Fula of the area, pagan and peaceful, and the Mandingo had easily conquered them. Many Jola states were now ruled by Mandingo.

The European missionaries who arrived in the Gambia from 1821 onwards soon found that their task was more difficult than they had expected, for they had to compete for converts with Muslim missionaries. And whereas some of the Muslim sects were not very zealous, others, like the Marabout, were fanatical in their devotion to their faith and their efforts to win adherents to it.

Expansion of the Gambia

As in the Gold Coast, the methods used by the British to establish and extend their authority over these native communities were the exploiting of local feuds and the extensive bribing or intimidation of local rulers. In 1823, for example, the British 'obtained' MacCarthy Island, 150 miles upriver, by offering Kolli, King of Kataba, protection against a rival king. They then built Fort George on the island, and so established permanent British control over it. Three years later a

The Nineteenth Century: Gambia, Sierra Leone and the Gold Coast

warship, H.M.S. *Maidstone*, and a steamer, the *African*, were used by Macaulay, Acting Governor of Sierra Leone, to frighten the King of Barra into 'granting' the British sovereignty over the whole waterway and its right bank in exchange for an annual 'payment'. Next year (1827) Governor Neil Campbell used another local quarrel between kings to obtain from the King of Wuli the 'grant' to Britain of Brikama on the other bank. This king also 'gave' the British sovereignty over Fattatenda.

It is true that this gradual extension of the British occupation of the Gambia was the work of local Governors and Lieutenant- Governors rather than the policy of the British Government in London. It is also true that it was not the wish of the people of the Gambia, however much it may have suited the temporary purpose of a short-sighted king here and there. In the 1830s Lieutenant-Governor Rendall had to fight major wars against the kings of Barra and Kataba, who were trying to preserve their sovereignty against the British. Barra lost its war, but Kataba defied the British guns successfully.

Gradually, however, the British extended their rule in the Gambia. In 1834 Deer Island and in 1840 Kombo were 'acquired' for the growing number of 'liberated Africans' being sent to Bathurst from Freetown. In 1841 the King of Kataba at last signed a treaty of protection with the British, not because of a military defeat by them, but in gratitude for their support in a war against the King of Kemintang and his Fula allies. Acting Governor Ingram was stopped from making more treaties with kings on the upper reaches of the river in 1842 only by bitter fighting between two Muslim sects in the area, the Marabout and Soninke; but a war between the people of Wuli and Bondu in 1843 led to the establishment of British rule over Bondu.

The Gambia gains a separate administration

In 1843 the demand for the creation of a separate administration for the Gambia succeeded, and an Act of the British Parliament in that year gave the colony its own Governor, Legislative and Executive Councils, and Judiciary. The Councils consisted entirely of officials, the Chief Justice, Colonial Secretary, General Officer Commanding and a Justice of the Peace being the members of the Legislative Council, and the Colonial Secretary, Collector of Customs and Queen's Advocate the members of the Executive Council. Henry Frowde Seagram was the first Governor. This change, however, did not make British administration any more popular with the indigenous people of the Gambia. The Governor's expedition to Kunnong near Tendeba in 1849 was fiercely attacked, in reply to which the British sent a heavily armed punitive expedition to raid the town.

The rest of the century is marked by two major developments in the Gambia. The warfare between the Muslim sects, which had frustrated Ingram in 1842, began to spread. The two leading opponents were the Soninke and Marabout, and so bitter was the fighting that the traditional British attempts to make use of the situation proved more costly than successful. Moreover, a yellow-fever epidemic at one stage reduced the number of Europeans left alive in the Gambia to ten. When Governor d'Arcy suggested the creation of a protectorate reaching far inland along both banks of the river, the British Government decided to set up a Select Committee to review its whole policy in West Africa.

The effect of the Report of the Select Committee of 1865

This committee's Report, submitted in June 1865, is a surprisingly early foreshadowing of the later policy of Britain to lead her colonies towards self-government. The Report recommended that no further colonies should be annexed, and that the administration of the British colonies in West Africa, divided in 1824 and 1843, should be united once more under the Governor of Sierra Leone. It added that with the possible exception of Sierra Leone (no reason is given for this exception) it should be the aim 'to encourage in the natives the exercise of those qualities which may render it possible for us to transfer to them more and more the administration of all the Governments, with a view to our ultimate withdrawal from all'. The recommendation about the uniting of the colonies was carried out; it took nearly a century for the British Government to carry out that about self-government.

This committee also recommended the withdrawal of the British garrison from MacCarthy Island, which island a devoted Sierra Leonean doctor, the only official left there, had to administer single-handed. Indeed the British were seeking to reduce their responsibilities all over the coast at this time, and were about to accept a French offer to exchange the Gambia for Dahomey (against violent opposition from the people of Bathurst), when the offer was withdrawn (1876).

Although the Gambia continued to have difficulties, such as a disastrous outbreak of cholera in 1869 which started on MacCarthy Island and killed 1,162 of the 4,000 people of Bathurst, and the continued Soninke-Marabout fighting, by 1869 the Gambia's surplus was helping to meet the deficit shown by the Gold Coast administration. Then in 1875 Musa Molloh, son of Alfa Molloh, a powerful Fula king, attacked the Mandingo Jola kingdoms along the south bank of the river. And when the Soninke-Marabout wars ended in that year with the forcible conversion by the Marabout leader and slave dealer, Fodi Kabba, of the Soninke king, Bojang, into a Marabout, another long struggle opened, this time between Musa Molloh and Fodi Kabba.

The Gambia regains a separate administration

Before then, however, the Gold Coast and Lagos colonies had been separated administratively from Sierra Leone (1873), and in 1888 Gambia recovered the administrative independence which she had enjoyed from 1843 to 1865. The

The Nineteenth Century: Gambia, Sierra Leone and the Gold Coast

following year (1889) treaties signed at Kansala between the Governor and the rulers of sixteen Jola towns and of Bintang and Central Kiang, all of whom were seeking British protection against the formidable Fodi Kabba, enabled an Anglo-French Commission to map out the boundaries of the Gambia in 1890-1. Britain now claimed sovereignty in the Gambia over 150,000 people living on 4,000 square miles, instead of the 14,000 people living on the seventy square miles on St Mary's, James and MacCarthy Islands and the small mainland pockets which she had formerly governed. In 1892 Fodi Kabba was defeated; in 1894 a protectorate was formally declared over the kingdoms within the newly extended boundaries, and the slave trade (although not slavery itself) made illegal within these kingdoms. At last the Gambia had found its modern shape. It appeared to have been pacified after fifty years of Soninke-Marabout and Fula-Marabout fighting. In 1895 the West India Regiment, which had been sent by Britain to keep the peace in the Gambia, was withdrawn.

b. SIERRA LEONE

The Colony under Governor MacCarthy and the coming of the missionaries

When we last looked at Sierra Leone the slave trade had just been banned, the Temne War of 1801—7 and company rule had both just ended, and the British Crown Colony had been established. Two thousand immigrants, some Nova Scotians, some Maroons, and perhaps a very few survivors of the original 411 settlers, lived in what is today the central part of Freetown, from Joaque Bridge to East Street. The Temne had lost the rest of the northern shore of this peninsula to the colonists, as well as Port Loko to the Susu. The latter were, however, forced in 1815 to return Port Loko to the Temne.

Trade was at first promising — and we must remember that it was trade the sponsors of the colony were seeking. As in the Gambia, timber became an important export at this time. To the south-east, on the Gallinas coast, some slave traders defied the ban up to 1850, but were finding it increasingly difficult to do so, as the British Navy patrolled the coast more and more thoroughly. Politically, the colony was ruled in the name of the British Crown by a Governor, who was advised by a council of senior officials. Between 1821, when the Company of Merchants' interests in the Gambia and the Gold Coast were taken over by the British Crown, and 1827, when a separate administration was set up in the Gold Coast, the Governor was responsible for these other territories as well as for Sierra Leone. The Gambia was not separated from Sierra Leone until 1843.

Social problems were developing in Freetown, however. More and more 'liberated Africans' were being brought in by the patrolling men-of-war and released in Freetown by the Admiralty court. An attempt was made to resettle them in nearby villages, but the arrangements made were not efficient. As a result, many of them took to crime or begging, and some of these were deported to the Gambia, as we have seen (page 12). Missionaries came to help with some of these problems, one of the first to arrive in Freetown being the Methodist, the Rev. George Warren (1811). The Church Missionary Society went first to the Rio Pongas (part of modern Guinea), and later to Freetown and the villages around, where they founded churches, schools and colleges, including Regent Church (1816), the Christian Institution at Leicester (1814), later to become Fourah Bay College, and secondary schools for boys (1845) and girls (1849). In 1852 the Anglican Diocese of Sierra Leone was founded (see page 14), and seven years later Roman Catholic missionaries arrived.

Relations with neighbouring kingdoms and European powers were now fairly good. The Temne gave up the York, Kent, Wellington, Hastings and Waterloo areas to ex-servicemen and 'liberated Africans' from the colony, and the Sherbro did the same with the Bananas. The Fula at Futa Jallon and Yalunka at Falaba received courtesy calls from Governor MacCarthy's representatives. An inscription on an old cannon outside the rest house at Lungi Airport reads: 'This cannon was presented by the British Government in 1822 to Chief Dala Modu of Bullom for his co-operation in maintaining peace. . . .'

Expansion of the Colony

Judges from other European countries sat with British judges in the Court of Mixed Commission in Freetown to enforce the ban on the slave trade. After Governor MacCarthy was killed fighting the Asante in the Gold Coast in 1824 (page 26), his successors settled quarrels amongst the Sherbro of the Plantain Islands and Temne of Port Loko (1825), and between the Temne on the one hand and the Loko and Mende on the other (1831). But the latter settlement was only temporary, and it was the Temne themselves who ten years later settled the matter finally by defeating the Loko at Kasona on the Mabole River. The Loko were dispersed to the north across the Mabole, and the Temne completed the rebuilding of their power which they had begun when they recovered Port Loko from the Susu in 1815 (page 17).

Within the colony itself another group was building their power — the 'liberated Africans'. Dispersed at first amongst the villages outside Freetown, they had gradually shown even more initiative and enterprise than the other settlers, and outstripped them in wealth and influence. This achievement is yet another tribute to Negro willpower and adaptability. They elected their own headmen, formed their own co-operative societies called 'companies', built their own mosques, churches and schools, opened their own shops and businesses. Some of them were Yoruba, who came to be known as Akus; others were Ibo, yet others Asante. The most enterprising of them moved from the villages first to Freetown, and then, when they had acquired enough wealth, down the coast and back to their own people. Sometimes there were violent quarrels between them. One of these, at Christmas 1843, led to a riot at Waterloo, twenty miles east of

The Nineteenth Century: Gambia, Sierra Leone and the Gold Coast

Freetown, which resulted in the setting up of a committee representing all the seventeen nations from which the settlers there originally came.

South of the colony, the Mende were continuing their movement towards the coast, and the Sherbro in some areas were adopting the Mende language and becoming dependent on the skilful Mende soldiers for protection. Relations between the British authorities in the colony and the kings of the surrounding country deteriorated during the second half of this century. The most important reason for this was the practice which we noted in the Gold Coast in the previous century by which the British persuaded African rulers to put their thumbprints to 'treaties' they could not understand fully. The Africans thought they were forming alliances for mutual protection between equal partners, which would involve temporary occupation of part of their land by their ally. They believed, therefore, they were doing no more than the British do today when they allow the Americans to set up military bases in Britain. When they discovered that they had in fact been tricked into 'agreeing' to give up their sovereignty over their land for good, they naturally attacked the British. This was how in 1861 Governor Hill 'acquired' Sherbro and British Koya, and why the end of the nineteenth century was so disturbed in Sierra Leone.

Another cause of friction was 'British gunboat imperialism' — a tendency to show off British power by blasting away with cannon at helpless villages at the smallest provocation. This happened in the Gambia in 1849 and again in Kambia in Sierra Leone in 1858 and 1859. It was probably in revenge for this that the Temne attacked and expelled the C.M.S. missionaries at Magbela in 1860. These had opened their first mission to the Temne at Port Loko twenty years before. The American missionaries who had started work on the Jong River in Mende country at about the same time, with the help of some Mende ex-slaves from Cuba, were not attacked at this time, as they were not associated with the British. Nor were the American missionaries of the United Brethren in Christ Church who had opened a mission in Shenge in Sherbro country in 1855.

Administrative development

In political matters the colony made very slow progress indeed. The Governor's Council had been given its first non-official member in 1811; but for the following fifty years nothing was done to give back to the people of the colony at least some of the control over their own affairs which they had lost when the Province of Freedom was destroyed in 1789. Governor Hill, who was in power at the end of those fifty years, did not wish to consult anyone when carrying out his duties; and it was only when Governor Blackhall succeeded him that Sierra Leone was given, in 1863, an Executive Council and a Legislative Council, which the Gambia had obtained twenty years before. The Executive Council had an entirely official membership, the Legislative Council had two non-official members as well as officials. The first two non-official members were wealthy traders: Charles Heddle, a mulatto who had been a member of the old council and whose farm is today an ancient monument well worth visiting, and John Ezzidio, a 'liberated African' from what is now Northern Nigeria. Both were appointed to the Legislative Council by the Governor (not elected); but Blackhall, being a far-sighted man, appointed Ezzidio on the nomination of his fellow traders in Freetown.

Although the British Secretary of State was not happy that Blackhall had asked these traders to make a nomination, the new constitution worked smoothly. Sierra Leone's laws had to be approved in London. The British valued their colony in Sierra Leone, and the 1865 Select Committee which recommended the reuniting of the four colonies foresaw ultimate independence only for the other three. When the united administration broke up again, Gambia once more was left linked to Sierra Leone longer than the others — Lagos and the Gold Coast broke away in 1874, Gambia in 1888. The mid-1860s also saw the capture of the last slave ships which tried to evade the watchful naval patrols off the West African coast.

The administrative merging of the other British West African colonies with and under Sierra Leone in 1821 and 1865 had one unfortunate effect on the people of Freetown. They formed the habit of looking along the coast instead of into the interior. One cannot blame them. Their ancestors mostly came from along the coast; most of the 'liberated Africans' actually spoke Joloff, Twi, Fante, Yoruba, Ibo or Hausa, not Mende or Temne; mailboats linked Bathurst, Freetown, Cape Coast and Lagos much more closely from 1852 onwards (when a regular service began) than Freetown, Kabala and Bo were linked.

The Creole community

So the descendants of the original settlers, the Nova Scotians, the Maroons and the 'liberated Africans', all gradually merged into one 'Creole' community in Freetown and its surrounding villages. Most of the members of that community tended in their way of life to turn their backs on the hinterland and gaze out to sea. Their diet and cookery borrowed heavily from that of the people of the Gold Coast and Nigeria, as did the women's dress fashions. Men's fashions were borrowed from Britain, as was education. Fourah Bay College was affiliated to Durham University in 1876. A language, Krio, emerged which borrowed from both Europe and Africa. Christianity, Islam and indigenous African cults were to be found together in Freetown, sometimes separate, sometimes curiously blended.

But in their trading the Creoles could not afford to ignore the interior. They aroused the resentment of many kings by travelling widely in the Scarcies area, in Mende country, and in Sherbro country, in search of customers for the imported goods they bought from the big firms which were beginning to establish themselves in Freetown. They were in search too of agricultural produce,

The Nineteenth Century: Gambia, Sierra Leone and the Gold Coast

particularly groundnut and palm oil-seeds, to sell to those firms for export to Europe. (Timber had become exhausted by this time.) The chiefs felt that these traders, whose way of life was entirely foreign to them, were displacing them as middlemen between their own people and the Europeans on the coast. This feeling was soon to lead to serious trouble, which even the praiseworthy but unsuccessful efforts of Christian Creole missionaries amongst the Temne and Limba could not avert.

For the time being, however, as in the Gambia between 1823 and 1841 and again in 1889 (pages 14-15), Britain was using gunboats and thumbprints to settle boundaries. In 1861 'British Sherbro' was 'acquired' by Governor Hill. In 1882 both the Scarcies and the Moa rulers were persuaded to accept British 'friendship' and protection. The modern coastal boundaries of Sierra Leone with Guinea and Liberia were taking shape, but not before Governor Havelock had sailed in a gunboat to Monrovia to intimidate the freed slaves from the American colonies who, having settled temporarily in Sherbro in 1818, had moved to Monrovia in 1821, and had made their Declaration of Independence in 1847.

Wars with neighbouring kings

During the second half of the century there was a series of wars. First the kings who felt their interests threatened by the Creole traders began to oppose all foreign traders; and by foreign they meant anyone not of their own people. The Yoni attacked the missionaries and traders on the Rokel in 1860 and again in the 1870s, then turned in 1883 on the Fula traders who had settled under a Loko chief at Rotifunk, and two years later on the Loko at Songo. This was the most daring of their attacks, as Songo, being within 'British Koya', had since 1861 been claimed by the British Crown. Governor Rowe went after the Yoni to try to punish them for this, but was unable to catch up with them; and in 1887 they attacked the famous woman ruler Madame Yoko of Senehun. Although the Creoles tried to persuade Rowe to extend the Crown Colony over the areas where recent treaties of 'friendship' had been signed, the Secretary of State in London would not allow this. If it was possible to have the advantages of trade with 'friendly' kings without the cost of administering their country, Britain preferred this.

But trade rivalry was leading to fighting in many parts of the hinterland by now. Some Mende kings led by Bokari Gomna attacked the Massaquoi of Sulima in the 1870s. Then in 1887 Sulima, another outpost of the colony, was attacked. Most unsettling of all perhaps was the appearance in Sierra Leone of the Sofa cavalry of the powerful Mandingo king, Samori, the great enemy of the French on the Niger. Using arms bought in Freetown, he helped the King of Kaliere to besiege Falaba in the 1880s. In Sherbro country it seemed that every time a Caulker king died a violent dispute followed over the succession, and the nearby Mende and the colonial authorities were usually on different sides.

West Africa in History

The British officials in Freetown were still forbidden by their superiors in London to extend their direct rule. But they decided to try to restore peace, and so trading prosperity, in the hinterland, by a show of force. The attacker of Sulima had been a powerful war-leader called Makaia from an area forty miles inland. In 1888 British troops allied with kings on the Kittam River and defeated Makaia, who fled to Panguma. By helping King Nyagua of Panguma against his enemies the British persuaded him to give Makaia up to them. They then deported Makaia to the Gold Coast. As more and more treaties of 'friendship' were signed with inland rulers, such as Kai Lundu of Kailahun, Frontier Police were posted in the rulers' towns to keep the peace, and to make sure the French did not extend their influence too near to the now valuable British naval base at Freetown.

The creation of the Protectorate and the rising of 1898

In 1895, after some skirmishes, the British and French agreed on Sierra Leone's boundaries, and a railway was started to link Freetown with the boundary directly east of it — the first railway in British West Africa. In 1896, as in the Gambia in 1894, a British protectorate was formally declared over the whole area agreed with the French as being 'British'.

Two years later, in 1898, the people of the Protectorate rose against the government and people of the colony. There were many causes for this. We have already seen that the Creole traders were disliked by the kings. The Frontier Police were unpopular too, for many of them bullied the kings and people instead of protecting them. The new protectorate administration was most unpopular of all, for two reasons: first it was mainly in the hands of district commissioners who had previously been unpopular Frontier Police officers, and who it now appeared to the kings were going to curtail their political power; second, in order to pay the costs of administering the Protectorate, Governor Cardew tried to raise a tax of five shillings, or its equivalent in rice or palm kernels, on each house in the Protectorate.

To kings and people it was now clear that they might lose economic power to the Creole traders, military power to the Frontier Police, political power to the district commissioners, and property rights (for they thought of the house tax as a form of rent) to the Governor in Freetown. Cardew made an extensive tour of the Protectorate to explain his plans, and ignored the protests the kings made and the advice the Creoles gave. Bai Bureh, a Loko king with powerful and disciplined Temne, Limba and Mende following, who had been arrested by the British for warring and had later helped them to put down other war-lords (1892), struck the first blow near Port Loko when in February 1898 the District Commissioner tried to collect the tax there. Then, organized by the Poro secret society, the Mende rose as one man on April 27, 1898, and turned not only on the government officials, as Bai Bureh's men had done, but on Creoles, Americans and

The Nineteenth Century: Gambia, Sierra Leone and the Gold Coast

Europeans, whether they were missionaries, traders, or officials, murdering as many as they could. Only after British and West Indian troops had launched a full-scale military operation was the rising put down. Many hundreds of people on both sides lost their lives, including ninety-six who were hanged in Freetown for their part in the rising. Bai Bureh, like Makaia, was deported to the Gold Coast, and so were Nyagua of Panguma and Be Sherbro of Yoni. The West African Frontier Force was formed to replace the West India Regiment, and marched through the Protectorate to demonstrate the strength of British rule in Sierra Leone. A special commissioner, Sir David Chalmers, reported to London that the rising had been provoked by the house tax. Yet in spite of this Cardew persuaded his superiors to let him continue with his proposal to collect this tax. The people of the Protectorate now paid up quietly, knowing that they had no defence against rifle-fire.

The Freetown Municipality

In 1895 the Freetown Municipality was created, the first Mayor being Sir Samuel Lewis. This provided a valuable training in government, and was in many ways the first step towards self-government for Sierra Leone.

C. THE GOLD COAST
The rivalry of the Asante and the Fante

The rivalry between Asante and Fante on the Gold Coast, which we saw coming to a head for the first time in 1765 and again in 1792, grew much more serious in the nineteenth century. The British were usually allies of the Fante, and the Dutch of the Asante.

At the beginning of 1806 the Asantehene charged some people with robbing graves. The Fante promptly gave refuge to the accused, who were people from Assin, and the Asantehene Osei Bonsu sent an army against the Fante. At Abora, four miles from Cape Coast, a big battle was fought, in which the Asante were successful. The British Company's agent at Cape Coast sheltered the accused grave robbers, whilst the Asante went on to attack the fort at Kormantine (Fort Amsterdam) of their old allies the Dutch. The British then tried to make friends with the Asante, and Colonel Torrane, who was in charge at Cape Coast, most treacherously handed an old and blind Assin king called Kwadwo Otibu to the Asantehene, although he knew that the old man would be killed; which he was.

A verbal agreement was now made between the British and the Asante that the latter should be recognized as the rulers of the Fante, except where a British fort existed. Shamelessly, Torrane sold or gave away 2,000 of his former Fante allies, and the Asante victoriously marched first east along the coast and then north back to their capital.

In 1811 the Asante moved south again, in response to an appeal for help from the people of Elmina, who were being attacked by the Fante. This time it was the

Asante who were let down by their allies. The state of Akim Abuakwa, which had promised to help them, suddenly supported the Fante. A big battle was fought, the Asante being supported by the Ga people of Accra as well as those of Elmina, against the Fanti-Akim alliance, which was joined by the Akwapim. The Asante won the pitched battle, but then had to retreat in the face of the guerilla tactics used by the Akwapim in the Akwapim Hills, where the Asante had the disadvantage of not knowing the terrain so well. The jubilant Akwapim, like the Asante in 1806, tried their new-found strength against the Europeans. They took a Dutch fort at Apam and a British one at Tantamkweri.

In 1814 the Asante again defeated the Akim-Akwapim alliance, but when they followed up their victory by pillaging Accra, instead of attacking the Europeans, they lost a valuable ally in the Ga people. Nevertheless, in 1816 they went on into Fante country, captured and killed the fleeing Akim Akwapim leaders and established themselves as overlords of all the region between the Asante and the sea.

The Company of Merchants and the Asante

The British Company of Merchants at Cape Coast watched the establishment of Asante supremacy with some misgivings. The French wars and the banning of the slave trade had already drastically cut the Company's profits. In 1817 the Company sent agents to make a treaty of friendship with the Asantehene, under which both sides undertook to promote peaceful trade on the Gold Coast. William Hutchinson was appointed the Company's permanent 'Resident' in Kumasi, and two years later he was joined there by a representative of the British Government, a consul.

The first consul, Joseph Dupuis, persuaded the Asantehene to sign a fresh treaty, this time with the British Government. By this the people of Cape Coast, although Fante, were exempted from the overlordship of the Asantehene. The Company's governor at Cape Coast, Mr Hope Smith, could see no reason for making this exemption, and would not consider himself bound by the treaty. Whilst Dupuis was in London trying to get the disagreement between himself and Hope Smith settled, the Asantehene became impatient at having to wait so long for ratification of the treaty. He ordered his subjects to trade with the Dutch and Danes instead of the British. The Company's fortunes had reached their lowest ebb, and it was with relief that in 1821 it handed its forts on the Gold Coast (Cape Coast, Anomabu, Accra, Beyin, Dixcove, Kommenda, Winneba, Sekondi, Prampram and Tantamkweri), like those in the Gambia, to the British Crown as represented by the Governor of Sierra Leone.

The Nineteenth Century: Gambia, Sierra Leone and the Gold Coast

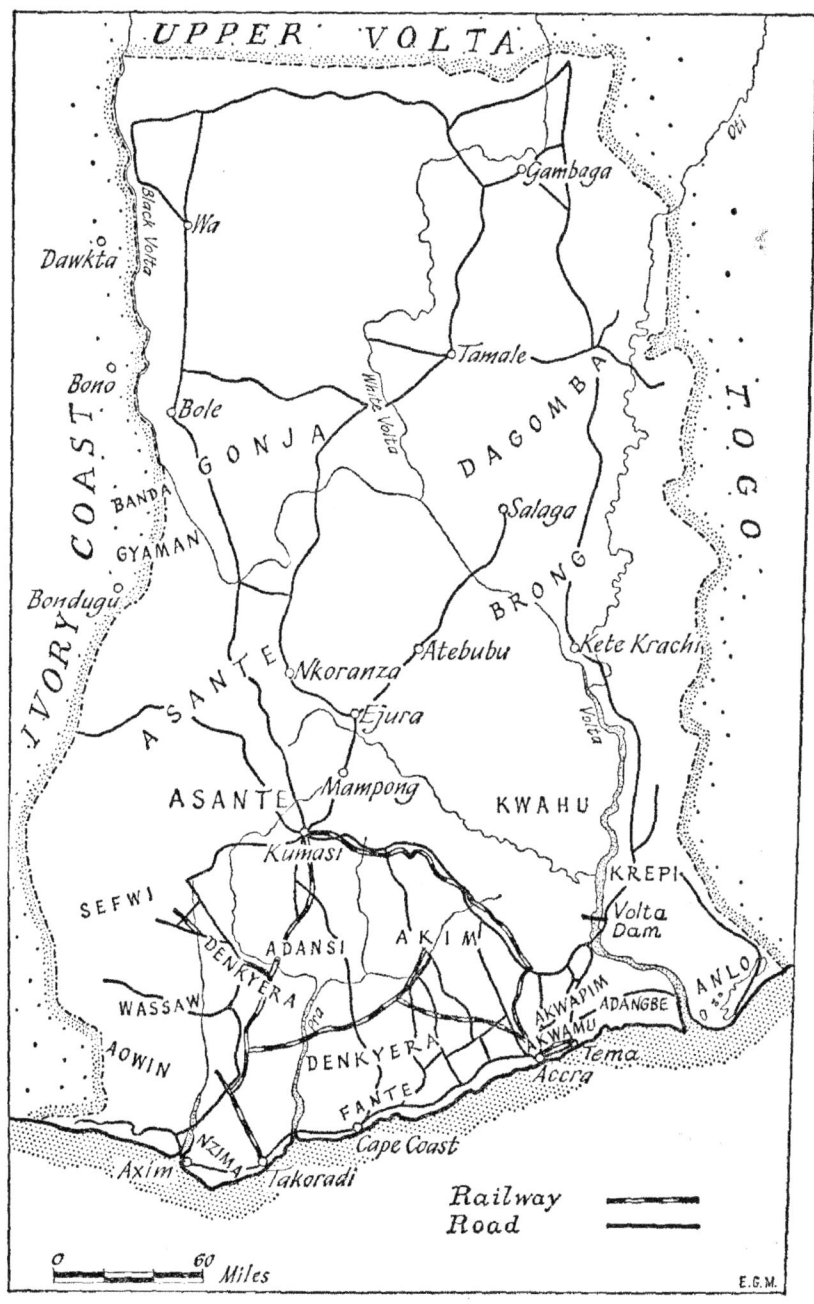

MAP 1 GHANA TODAY

The wars with the Asante 1824—6

The Governor there at this time was Sir Charles MacCarthy, who sailed to Cape Coast at once to survey his new responsibilities. He concluded that British interests in the Gold Coast required the crushing of the powerful Asantehene. But when, having returned to Sierra Leone briefly to collect troops, he faced the latter at the battle of Nsamankow (January 21, 1824), he was killed in battle, and the new governor was given charge of the Gold Coast alone.

By a strange chance, that same day the Asantehene, Osei Bonsu, died in Kumasi, and was succeeded by Osei Yaw Akoto. He maintained Asante resistance to the British by demanding that the latter give up Kwadwo Otibu of Denkyera, their ally and the enemy of the Asante. At another battle at Efutu a joint Denkyera and British force was defeated. But the Asante had now reached the highest point of their success. When they tried to storm the strongly fortified British headquarters at Cape Coast, they failed. Whilst they recovered their strength back in Asante during the next two years (1824—6), the British were building up a powerful alliance with the Fante, Ga, Akim and Denkyera people, all of whom were now thoroughly afraid of the Asante. It was this alliance which defeated the Asante army at the battle of Dodowa[1] on August 7, 1826. The new governor, Sir Neil Campbell, however, found the Asante still strong enough to refuse to sign any treaties.

The London Company of Merchants is made responsible for the settlements

The year 1828 was one of uncertainty as to the future of the British forts on the Gold Coast. Missionaries from Basle in Switzerland first came out to Christiansborg in that year to try to make converts, and so perhaps improve relations between Europeans and Africans. The British Government reasoned that if it withdrew from the scene a reconciliation between the merchants and peoples on the coast and the Asantehene might prove easier to make. It therefore gave instructions to the Governor of Sierra Leone, Sir Neil Campbell, that he should not make alliances with African peoples who would expect Britain to protect them, and gave orders that British officials and garrisons should be withdrawn from the Gold Coast forts. The forts, however, were to remain British territory, and the British Government paid the London Committee of Merchants £4,000 a year to maintain them. The settlements were to be governed by a Governor and an elected Council which was to have jurisdiction only over British forts and harbours and the people residing therein.

---

[1] Known as Katamanso or Akantamasu to Ghanaians.

The Nineteenth Century: Gambia, Sierra Leone and the Gold Coast

Captain George Maclean

In 1830 the London Committee sent out as President of the Council (or Governor) Captain George Maclean who, in 1831, came to terms with the Asante. He achieved this in spite of the fact that he had not any real power and little backing from the British government. Furthermore the attempts of the British government to come to terms with the Asante after Dodowa had been opposed by the coastal peoples, who feared that the Asante would again assert their claim to suzerainty over them. Even among the merchants there were some who thought Maclean should confine his activities and authority to those actually living within the British forts. By the terms of the treaty signed in 1831 by the Governor (Maclean) two Asante delegates, six Fante chiefs, representatives of Assin, Tufel and Denkyera and other African chiefs, the Asantehene paid the British 600 ounces of gold, gave two hostages from the royal family and recognised the independence of Denkyera and Assin. The gold and the hostages were later returned to Kumasi.

Maclean proved a man of outstanding personality and determination. He set about improving the economic position of the country and developed trade especially in palm oil. By establishing peace, he assisted the development of agriculture. He gained a reputation for impartiality as a judge which extended far beyond his limited official area. His position depended on his character and influence. At the same time it must be recognized that it was unlikely that the Asante would for long maintain the rather one-sided treaty of 1831. In 1838 when Kwaku Dua (1838—67) succeeded Osei Yaw Akoto as Asantehene he was persuaded to reopen the war against the Assin, Akim and Denkyera. Thus the uneasy seven-year peace ended—a time during which trade increased and Wesleyan missionary work was begun on the Gold Coast, thanks to Maclean's support.

Maclean in his work was hindered by the Danes at Christiansborg and the Dutch at Elmina. The former claimed control of Accra and were endeavouring to establish a protectorate over Akwapim, Akim and Krobo. The Dutch were suspected of intriguing with the Asante to resume the slave trade and of encouraging them to attack the coastal tribes again by supplying them with arms.

Hill succeeds Maclean

In 1843 the British government resumed the administration of the Gold Coast and appointed a Lieutenant-Governor, who was responsible to the Governor of Sierra Leone. Maclean remained as Judicial Assessor with special responsibility for the administration of justice among the coastal tribes. He sat in court with Fante chiefs and assisted in the trying of cases where Africans alone were involved and where Fante customary law was administered. He had no jurisdiction in matters concerning slavery. Maclean died in 1843, having done much to re-establish British reputation and authority. He had had many enemies who accused him of closing his eyes to slavery and the slave trade, of exceeding his authority and even of murdering his wife, but his reputation for impartiality helped the British to negotiate the Bond of 1844.

The Bond of 1844

It was Hill who negotiated the Bond of 1844, an important document in the history of the Gold Coast. Its chief effect was to legalize the vague protectorate that Maclean's personal influence had established. The terms of the Bond as quoted by Ward, *History of Ghana*, p. 194 (1966 edn.) are:,

1. Whereas power and jurisdiction have been exercised for and on behalf of Her Majesty the Queen of Great Britain and Ireland, within divers countries and places adjacent to Her Majesty's forts and settlements on the Gold Coast; we, chiefs of countries and places so referred to, adjacent to the said forts and settlements, do hereby acknowledge that power and jurisdiction, and declare that the first objects of law are the protection of individuals and property.
2. Human sacrifices, and other barbarous customs, such as panyarring[1] are abominations, and contrary to law.
3. Murder, robberies and other crimes and offences, will be tried and inquired of before the Queen's judicial officers and the chiefs of the districts, moulding the customs of the country to the general principles of British law.

Done at Cape Coast Castle before his Excellency the Lieutenant-Governor on this 6th day of March, in the year of our Lord,1844.

The document was signed by the Governor and eight chiefs including the Kings of the Fante, Denkyera, Assin, Anomabu, Dominase and Cape Coast people. Other chiefs signed later. Those who signed, like the Kings of the Gambia and Sierra Leone, probably believed they were consenting to an innocent treaty of friendship. In fact the Bond of 1844, in addition to banning human sacrifices and recognizing both British and African criminal law, had the effect of transferring sovereignty over the coastal areas of the Gold Coast to the British Crown. The British forts on the Gold Coast now became the British Crown Colony of the Gold Coast.

---

[1] *panyarring* the seizure of any fellow townsman of a debtor and holding him as a security. The family of the man thus panyarred would naturally put pressure on the original debtor to pay. During the slave trade there was a strong temptation to panyar a man for a small debt and sell him into slavery without giving his family a chance to secure payment of the debt; thus making a handsome profit (Ward, *History of Ghana*).

The Nineteenth Century: Gambia, Sierra Leone and the Gold Coast

The Gold Coast is separated from Sierra Leone — Danish forts purchased

In 1847 a third mission started work on this coast, the Bremen missionaries. In January 1850 the Gold Coast was separated from Sierra Leone, and given its own government with a Governor, Executive Council and nominated Legislative Council. Also in 1850 Britain purchased for £10,000 the Danish forts and settlements all of which lay to the east of Accra. The most important of these were Christiansborg and Keta. The chiefs concerned agreed to this transfer, and British influence spread further when more chiefs agreed to sign the Bond. The continued presence of the Dutch was, however, a difficulty, as they controlled Elmina, Axim, Sekondi, Accra, Butri, Shama, Kommenda, Mori, Kormantine and Apam.

Opposition to British rule grows

The 1850s and 1860s saw the beginning of active opposition by the people of the Gold Coast to the British rule which they now realized their Kings had admitted in 1844. The British authorities on the Gold Coast were in difficulties through lack of funds, as the grant by the British home government was inadequate. An assembly of chiefs, styling itself a legislative assembly, agreed that the people should pay taxes and voted a poll tax of one shilling a head for every man, woman and child. It was supposed to be used for improving the system of justice, providing more and better roads, extending education and medical aid, but in fact did little more than maintain the bribes (or stipends as they were called) to the Kings and chiefs. But it was soon found that the assembly had no right to agree to such a tax and the people also objected to its collection by the Governor's officers. The result was that it yielded little and was soon abandoned, but not before the people of Christiansborg, Teshi and Labadi had attacked Christiansborg Castle in protest against the tax, and had had their homes destroyed by the guns of the castle and of a man-of-war.

The Asante attack 1863

The Asante were outside the range of these guns, and when they set aside the 1831 agreement and invaded the British 'protectorate' they overcame the West India Regiment which was sent against them and won the battles of Asikuma and Bobikuma (1863) with the result that the British withdrew before them. The British government not wishing to commit itself further in West Africa would not allow the British governor Richard Pine to counter attack and the Asante brought trade to a standstill and British prestige to rock bottom.

The Select Committee's Report of 1865 and the Gold Coast

As a result of these events Colonel Ord was sent to inquire into and report on the four British West African colonies. A Select Committee of the House of Commons considered his report in 1865, and recommended that the British government should give up Lagos, Gambia and the Gold Coast and retain only Sierra Leone. The Committee, however, realized that Britain had too many obligations to merchants, missionaries and Africans to agree to these withdrawals immediately. It therefore recommended that the three other colonies be administered through Sierra Leone until the African states were ready for self-government. The British government put these recommendations into effect in 1865.

One immediate effect of these decisions was the limitation of British territory in the Gold Coast to Dixcove, Anomabu, Accra and Christiansborg and the land within five miles radius of Cape Coast Castle. This encouraged the Fante chiefs to think of organizing themselves so that they could resist any further Asante invasion. One chief, King Aggrey of Cape Coast, carried his new found independence too far by stirring up trouble and defying the British with the result that he was deported to Sierra Leone in 1866. There he was kept until he was allowed to return to Cape Coast as a private citizen in 1869. Before any effective organization could be set up, further serious conflict with the Asante developed.

Asante threat is renewed

In 1866 the British were drawn into a dispute between a slave dealer de Lema and his allies the Awuna (or Anlo) and the Ada. British gunboats and a force of Accra and Akwapim warriors aided the Ada, but disaster nearly overtook the allies at Datsutagba where the Akwapim saved the day. The government were tardy in putting peace terms to the Awuna and they entered into an alliance with the Asantehene Kwaku Dua. The Asante under a general named Nantwi invaded the country of the Krepi up the Volta, and once more menaced the Gold Coast 'protectorate'.

Anglo-Dutch Agreement and its effects

The British and the Dutch decided that the new Asante threat to their interests in the Gold Coast could only be met by consolidating their respective interests. They agreed to regard the Sweet River, between Elmina and Cape Coast, as the dividing line between these interests. The British handed their forts at Beyin, Dixcove, Sekondi and Kommenda to the Dutch and received in exchange the Dutch forts at Mori, Kormantine, Apam and Crevecoeur (later Ussher Fort). Thus the British were confined to the east, the Dutch to the west of Sweet River. The British hoped that by this arrangement they would be able to collect customs and other taxes on trade to pay for the proper administration of the country.

If anything, however, this arrangement increased the difficulties of the Europeans. The people of Beyin and Kommenda attacked the Dutch. In 1868 most of the Fante kings met at Mankessim and formed the Fante Confederation which agreed to help the people of Kommenda against the Dutch and their allies, the people of Elmina, who in their turn were in alliance with the Asante. It was not long before what looked like a simple transfer had brought about a large scale war, as the Assin, Wassaw and Denkyera joined the Fante. It was clear too that though the movement was chiefly against Elmina and the Dutch, with fear of the Asante in the background, there was also a move towards self-government. The fear of the Asante became all the greater when, in 1867, Kwaku Dua was succeeded as Asantehene by Kofi Karikari whose attitude was warlike and who offered help to Elmina which was now blockaded by the Fante.

The Asante army launched a three-pronged attack on the coast. Its western claw, making a wide sweep through Axim, and what is today the Ivory Coast, linked up successfully with its Elmina allies; the eastern claw, after being temporarily stopped by the Krepi people at Amedzofe, took Anum and Ho in 1869, and sent many prisoners, including a German missionary and his wife and child, another German missionary, and a French trader, back to Kumasi. For a time the acting British administrator, Mr W. H. Simpson, who was trying to smooth things out was held prisoner, but he was later released. The Asante, however, knew that they could not match the British guns so they halted their advance, while continuing to hold the missionaries and to claim Elmina as their possession, since the Dutch had always paid them some kind of rent for the fort. For the time being, therefore, hostilities petered out.

The Dutch give up their Settlements
The Dutch now were firmly resolved to give up their remaining forts and settlements and after somewhat long-drawn-out negotiations, the transfer of these to Britain was carried out in April 1872, without any real solution of the Asante claim to suzerainty over Elmina having been achieved.

The Mankessim constitution
Meanwhile the Fante kings and chiefs had not abandoned the idea of forming a Confederation with a definite constitution and on October 16, 1871, the Mankessim constitution of forty-seven articles was agreed. The objects of the Confederation were to promote the well-being of the people, to promote friendship among the kings and chiefs of the Fante and unity against their common enemy (the British), to improve education, communications, agriculture and the natural resources of the country. There was to be a King-President, and a representative assembly consisting of two representatives of each king and principal chief with legislative powers, an executive to carry out the wishes of the British government, and the power to levy taxes on the member states. The Mankessim constitution is a remarkable document, but it was never put into effect. The acting administrator at the time, Mr Salmon, on receiving a copy of the constitution for forwarding to the Governor-in-Chief in Sierra Leone, and thence to the Secretary of State, arrested the three officials of the Confederation who brought him the document and put them in prison. The Secretary of State tried to be tactful by saying that her Majesty's government had no wish to

discourage the efforts of the Fante kings and chiefs to establish an improved government 'but the protecting government must be consulted as to any new institutions which may be proposed'. Later he declared he had made up his mind on the Fante constitution but the present moment was inopportune for a discussion of it. A more favourable opportunity never arrived and so the Fante Confederation came to nought.

The 'Sagrenti' War 1873—4

In 1872 a new Governor-in-Chief, Mr Pope Hennessy, arrived in West Africa, and hoped to find a peaceful solution to the Asante question. He found two thorny problems, Elmina and the release of the missionaries. As Hennessy would not ransom the missionaries and Elmina was awaiting deliverance by the Asante, war broke out in January 1873 with the Asante attacking the 'protectorate'. The British this time resolved on really strong military action and sent out Major-General Sir Garnet Wolseley, known as Sagrenti to Africans, who, as well as being military commander, was appointed Civil Administrator. He arrived in October 1873, and gathered a force of British, West Indian and West African troops as well as marines and sailors to oppose the forces of the Asantehene. After preliminary engagements in which the Asante suffered heavy losses, Wolseley began a converging attack on Kumasi in January 1874, at the same time issuing the following armistice terms: an indemnity of 50,000 ounces of gold, the release of all prisoners and an escort of 500 men to accompany Sir Garnet to Kumasi for the signing of a formal treaty.

These terms were, of course, unacceptable to the Asante who put up a brave but unavailing resistance to the British and on February 4, 1874 Wolseley entered Kumasi which was deserted and already ablaze, possibly set on fire by the Fante prisoners whom the Asante had left behind. Finding no one with whom he could make a peace, Wolseley left Kumasi and retired towards the coast.

The Treaty of Fomena, February 1874, and its effects on Asante

Envoys from the Asantehene, Kofi Karikari, caught up with Wolseley at Fomena, and on February 12, 1874 agreed to a dictated peace, the chief terms of which were that the Asante should pay an indemnity of 50,000 ounces of gold, that the Asantehene should give up all claims to suzerainty over Denkyera, Assin, Akim, Adansi and Elmina, should keep the road from Kumasi to the Pra river clear for trade, and should do his best to stop human sacrifices. The treaty was signed on March 14, 1874. Some of the terms, e.g. the 50,000 ounces of gold, which the Asante could never produce, could not be fulfilled and thus the British were left with opportunities for future intervention. It soon seemed that the Asante Kingdom was collapsing. Kofi Karikari was deposed and succeeded by his younger brother Mensa Bonsu. Many of the subject states broke away - Juaben, Kwahu, Mampong, Agona, Nsuta, Bekwai, Kokofu, Brong, Techimang and Atabubu. He was only able to defeat Juaben before he in his turn was

The Nineteenth Century: Gambia, Sierra Leone and the Gold Coast

deposed in 1883. There followed five years of wars in Kumasi before Kwaku Dua III, more often known as Prempeh, was enstooled in 1888.

The Gold Coast again separated from Sierra Leone

In 1874, after Wolseley had left the Gold Coast, that territory was once more separated from Sierra Leone, the Governor now being also responsible for Lagos. One of the new Governor's first acts was to declare both slavery and slave trading illegal for all, not only Europeans, in the two colonies. The British position on the Gold Coast was strengthened by the acquisition of Keta and the area round it as a result of the Treaty of Dzelukofe with the Awuna. In 1879 the Anglican Church was founded in Accra and two years later the Roman Catholic Church started its missionary work at Elmina. Perhaps of greater significance for the Gold Coast's history was the bringing by Tetteh Quashie in 1879 of the first cocoa seeds from Fernando Po and São Tome.

Prempeh's deposition — Asante a Crown Colony

After Wolseley's victory and the Treaty of Fomena, the Gold Coast government followed a weak policy towards Asante, hoping to avoid any further war. They wanted the Asantehene to be just strong enough to hold Asante down, but to be without any threatening military power. The years after 1874 were taken up with minor differences between the British and Asante, and major troubles within Asante itself, which seemed to be resolved when Prempeh was firmly established as Asantehene.

In 1890 the British Governor of the Gold Coast, Sir Brandford Griffith, tried to persuade Prempeh to sign a treaty of 'friendship' and protection with him. But Gold Coast kings had at long last realized what these treaties led to. Prempeh, who was to prove one of the greatest of the Asantehenes, declined to sign. When he had defeated the hostile Nkoranza people in 1892, he felt strong enough to send messengers all the way to London to the British Queen to confirm that he was in no need of her protection. The British Governor asked Prempeh whether he would agree to talks being held between the two sides.

In April 1895, only a few days after the Asante mission had sailed for England, Mr William Maxwell arrived to take over the Governorship from Sir Brandford Griffith. On the instructions of the Secretary of State, he demanded that the Asantehene should receive a British Resident at Kumasi immediately and at the same time drew attention to the non-fulfillment of the terms of the Treaty of Fomena. The Asantehene, while apparently agreeing, endeavoured to draw the British delegation to Kumasi, possibly in the hope of trapping it, but instead he found himself faced by a strong expeditionary force which quickly reached Kumasi. Prempeh made some kind of submission to the Governor, and then claimed the protection of the Queen of England. The Asantehene, it seems, would have been acknowledged as Kumasihene, but he was arrested with the Queen Mother and most of the royal family. Prempeh was deported first to Sierra

Leone and in 1900 to the Seychelles. The British Governor, Sir Frederic Hodgson, made the blunder of coupling with excessive demands for gold a demand for the surrender of the Golden Stool which contained the soul of all Asante. His search for it was unavailing but stirred the people of Kumasi and their neighbours to action. They rallied under Yaa Asantewa, Queen Mother of Ejisu, to defend the seat of their nation's spirit. Governor Hodgson and his wife were forced to take refuge in the fort in Kumasi; the town was barricaded by its citizens against the British soldiers, most of whom were searching outside it for the Golden Stool. Fortunately for Governor Hodgson, he and his wife were able to escape, and a relief British army soon forced its way into Kumasi. That same year (1901) Asante was declared by the British one of their colonies, to be administered by the Governor of the Gold Coast.

The boundaries settled

Following the conquest of Asante Britain extended its sphere of influence northwards to forestall the advance of French and Germans. In the year 1898-9 agreements between the British, French and Germans decided the boundaries between the Gold Coast and the French Ivory Coast on one side, and German Togoland on the other. In the determining of these boundaries the colonial powers paid no attention to tribal or African political divisions.

The Lands Bill and the Gold Coast Aborigines' Rights Society

Before closing this section it would be well to turn back to the internal affairs of the Gold Coast. A Crown Lands Bill of 1894 which would have vested in the Queen 'all waste and forest land' aroused a great indignation and was dropped. It was followed in 1897 by the Lands Bill which aimed at controlling the concessions which were being made by chiefs and others. This too aroused opposition, and Joseph Chamberlain, then Colonial Secretary, dropped it. One of the most vigorous of the opponents of these measures was J. Mensah Sarbah, the first Gold Coast African to be called to the Bar, and there arose out of the agitation the Gold Coast Aborigines' Rights Society which soon had branches in most coastal towns and elsewhere, and which many chiefs joined. This Society did not prevent the passage through the Legislative Council of the Concessions Ordinance of 1900, but it had established itself as a voice of African opinion and a forerunner of more powerful national parties.

The agitation by the Aborigines' Rights Society was a continuation of the constitutional struggle against British rule in the Gold Coast which had been started by the Mankessim meetings and which, unlike the military struggle, the British were bound eventually to lose. Sarbah was a lawyer, and the new intellectuals were far better equipped for this struggle than the old kings. Instead of fighting the idea of empire with guns, they fought it with other, and better, ideas.

2
Nigeria in the Nineteenth Century

The West

The Yoruba Empire

In 1800 what became the Western Region of the Federation of Nigeria formed the heart of a Yoruba Empire which may have stretched from the Niger to Accra. Its capital was Oyo on the northern edge of the Empire, which was at its greatest strength in the first half of the eighteenth century. It showed signs of weakening in the latter part of the eighteenth century, especially during the reign of Abiodun. The Alafin of Oyo claimed to be a descendant of Oduduwa, the first Oni of Ife. Ife was acknowledged as the spiritual centre not only of Yorubaland but also more loosely of a much wider area, but it had lost political importance.

The break-up of the Yoruba Empire began about 1817, and thereafter there was civil war in Yorubaland for some seventy years. In 1817 Yoruba Ilorin, helped by the Fulani, shook off the Oyo yoke and a Fulani emirate was established there. In 1818 King Gezo of Dahomey whose ancestors had paid tribute to the Alafin declared his independence, using his powerful army, which included women soldiers, to overrun much of the country to the west of Oyo. The geographical position of Oyo made for weakness in the Empire as trade was now flowing southwards towards the coast instead of towards the traditional routes northwards, and, further, the forces of Islam were a constant threat.

By the year 1800 a decline in the slave trade along the coasts of Africa was setting in. The profits and activities of Britain far exceeded those of other countries, her chief rivals being Holland and France. By the end of the eighteenth century Britain needed crops like palm-oil grown in Africa by Africans as free men more urgently than crops like tobacco grown in America by Africans as slaves. The abolition of the slave trade by Britain in 1807 greatly speeded the decline. The biggest markets for the slave trade had been along the 'slave coast' between Porto Novo and Calabar. The slaves were brought from inland, often from the country round large towns. Moreover the civil wars among the Yoruba resulted in many women and men being taken prisoner and sent to the slave markets on the coasts whence they were shipped to America.

MAP 2 THE YORUBA EMPIRE

Civil wars in Yorubaland

There had, of course, been revolts and civil wars throughout the history of the Oyo Empire. In one such revolt an Egba leader named Lishabi defeated the Alafin Abiodun's army on the Ogun River in the 1770s and claimed independence for the Egba. The death of Lishabi was followed by civil war in the Egba country and this civil war became merged in the general upheaval in the Oyo Empire.

The Fulani were the real danger to the peoples of Western Nigeria in the first half of the nineteenth century. After having established themselves in Ilorin, they drove the Oyo refugees into Ijebu. The Ijebu had recently introduced the use of gunpowder into their warfare and they were the more powerful as they had additional reserves of manpower in Oyo refugees. Anxious to extend their power in 1821, the Ijebu attacked and destroyed Owu which itself had defeated Ife, the spiritual and cultural home of the Yoruba. The Owu fled to Egba towns for shelter and protection. As a result of the rise of Ijebu, the slave trade which had followed the Niger—Oyo—Porto Novo route, now interrupted by the Fulani at Ilorin, found a new channel to the sea between Ijebu and Lagos. Growing in strength, the Ijebu Oyo allies destroyed several Egba towns between 1821 and 1826, and in about 1830 the Egba founded Abeokuta as a city of refuge.

The founding of Ibadan

The history of Ibadan and Abeokuta interlocks during this period. At the beginning of the nineteenth century Ibadan was a small village of Gbagura people. Its name was probably derived from 'Eba-Oban', 'on the edge of the open grass country', which describes its site. It developed into a fairly large town under Lagelu from Ile-Ife and its importance was recognized by the Alafin Songo of Oyo who appointed Lagelu 'Jagun (Sword) of the Yoruba'. The people of Ibadan, however, made the error of mocking the Egungun cult, which so incensed nearby Obas that they destroyed the town. Lagelu escaped to a hill called Oke-Ibadan where he refounded his town on the present site. This new town was annexed by the Gbagura, a branch of the Egba, and it was here that the first all-Egba military command was formed.

During the Owu war of 1821, Ibadan shared the fate of the Gbagura towns and was invaded by the Ijebu and their allies. The people of Ibadan led by Sodeke withdrew across the river Ona, leaving Maye, the great Ife warrior, who was leading the Ijebu, Ife and Oyo forces, to occupy their town, and to admit hundreds of Oyo and Egba refugees from the Fulani.

The founding of Abeokuta

Sodeke and his followers were not left in peace for long, and, on being attacked by the new occupants of Ibadan, they moved south and founded Abeokuta, 'under the Olumo Rock'. Under the leadership of Sodeke they built a wall round their new town, and in their turn admitted refugees. It was as well they did, for the Ijebu attacked them again in the Owiwi War of 1832. With the help of King Adele of Lagos they beat off this attack, fell on the Egbado allies of the Ijebu, and having captured the Egbado capital Ilaro placed a pro-Egba ruler on the Egbado throne. Sodeke was now recognized as Balogun (war-captain), but he wisely exercised his power through the Ologun or war-chiefs who were also Muslim leaders and so doubly powerful. Abeokuta was made up of several communities, the Egba Alake, the Egba-Oke-Ona, the Gbagura and the Owu refugees, who all formed a kind of federation under the leadership of Sodeke.

Ibadan-Abeokuta rivalry

From 1834 onwards Abeokuta was under almost constant attack by the Egbado and by Oyo, Ijebu and Ibadan. The latter was now ruled by an Oyo civil government, following the execution of Maye. In 1835 Abeokuta and Ibadan fought the Arakonga war. The former, still under the leadership of Sodeke, won it with the assistance of Owu refugees. Following this, more and more refugees flocked to Abeokuta, including in 1839 Egba ex-slaves liberated in Freetown by the International Court of Mixed Commission set up for this purpose. Most of these freed slaves were Christian, and in 1842 they asked the British Church Missionary Society for a missionary. As a result the Anglican missionary Henry Townsend arrived in Abeokuta in 1850.

Sodeke the founder of Abeokuta died in 1845. His last campaign was against the town of Ado which was in alliance with Gezo, King of Dahomey. When the latter went to the assistance of Ado, Sodeke drove him off and affronted him by seizing his war charms, umbrella and stool. It was not until 1853 that the Egba siege of Ado was raised, following missionary intervention. The most persistent cause of rivalry and civil war in Yorubaland was interference with trade and access to the sea. Abeokuta lay on one of Ibadan's trade routes to Lagos, and the Dahomey frequently threatened the routes of both Abeokuta and Ibadan.

Both Ibadan and Abeokuta re-organized their government about this time. In Ibadan Oluyedun, a member of the Afonja princely house, became the first Are Ona Kakanfo of Ibadan. Oluyole, the most powerful figure, an Oyo and the grandson of an Alafin, became Basorun, a title conferred on him by Atiba the Alafin and founder of modern Oyo. He developed its agriculture by encouraging the growing of yams and kola nuts.

In Abeokuta, Ayikondi, Balogun of Igbein succeeded Sodeke as Balogun of all the Egba whilst Apati held the title of Basorun and led the pro-Kosoko party which, as we shall see, brought about the expulsion of King Akitoye of Lagos who had taken shelter there after his flight in 1845. Largely through the influence of Townsend the title of Alake was revived, the holder claiming descent from Oduduwa, like the Alafin of Oyo. Abeokuta, like other Egba towns, had an Ogboni Society of influential men and women who acted as an electoral College, and a Parakoyi Society which served as a chamber of commerce.

In spite of the arrival of missionaries in Abeokuta, slaving still continued. Abaka was raided for slaves in 1846, and most of the Ologun or war-chiefs, who were as we have seen Muslims, were also slave traders. To their credit it must be said that some of them forbade the persecution of the Christians of Abeokuta. However, the missionary Townsend did not feel he could rely on their continuing to restrain the persecutors; and in 1848 he personally asked Queen Victoria for more teachers and missionaries for Abeokuta, and furthermore asked the British Queen to accept responsibility for the protection of the teachers and missionaries and their converts. The Queen agreed to put the matter before her ministers.

The 1850s saw more warfare in both Ibadan and Abeokuta. In Ibadan Oluyole, who was a shrewd and restless despot, died in 1846. His death was followed by a period of confusion and divided authority as well as war with Ijaiye.

Then in 1859 the Alafin Atiba, founder of new Oyo and overlord of both Ibadan and Ijaiye, died. According to Oyo custom Adelu, the Aremo or Crown Prince, should have committed suicide or been put to death, but instead he was elected Alafin. Kurunmi Are Ona Kakanfo of Ijaiye refused to recognize Adelu as Alafin and the Ibadan army was ordered to bring him to heel. As a result war broke out in spite of a British attempt to prevent it. The Ijaiye were defeated, although they had Egba help, and the war ended in 1864. Ibadan's leaders were Ibikule and Ogunmola, who became Basorun. The Egba of Abeokuta had their worries too in the 1850s. In 1850 Gezo, King of Dahomey, helped by the exiled King Kosoko of Lagos and King Possu of Badagry, prepared to go to war against Abeokuta to recover his umbrella, war charms and stool. With an army, said to number 10,000 men and 6,000 women, he attacked Abeokuta in March 1851. The Anglican missionary Townsend and the Baptist Bowen assisted in the defence of Abeokuta, which was also given valuable help by the Egbado people of Ishaga. Both sides suffered many casualties before Abeokuta gained the advantage.

British intervention grows

European missionary interference in local struggles in Western Nigeria was quickly followed by interference by European governments. The British helped the Egba to improve the defences of Abeokuta whilst the Dahomey were helped by the French. The British were rewarded by the assistance of the Egba in the restoration of the puppet King Akitoye to the throne of Lagos in 1851.

In 1862, after the annexation of Lagos by Britain in 1861, the new Governor, H. Stanhope Freeman, tried to use a Dahomey attack on Ishaga near Abeokuta as an opportunity to persuade the Egba to accept a British Vice-Consul in Abeokuta, but he was unsuccessful, as the Egba did not wish to have a permanent British representative in their city, whatever the military advantage might be. Moreover neither the missionaries in Abeokuta nor the Colonial Office in London shared Freeman's expansionist views. He had to content himself with annexing Palma, Lekki and Badagry to the Lagos colony, and destroying Epe. In 1864 the Dahomey, under a new King Gelele, attacked Abeokuta again and followed this by an attack on Ikorodu. Both attacks failed, the British again showing their willingness to give the Egba assistance.

Abeokuta suffered at this time from weak government. The revival of the office of Alake in 1854 (Okukenu the Sagbua was appointed to it) did not strengthen the government much. At the same time the trade of the town flourished, and the missionaries helped the economy by encouraging agriculture including the growing of cotton. In 1865 an official report by a Parliamentary Select Committee led to the banning of any further extension of British power in West Africa for the time being, thus restricting the activities of British officials in Lagos. An example of the power of these officials is the expulsion in 1856 of Madame Tinubu from Lagos on the insistence of the British Consul, Campbell. She was a prominent trader in salt and tobacco and objected to the competition of 'emancipados' or freed slaves from Brazil, Cuba and Sierra Leone. King Dosunmu drove her out and she settled in Abeokuta where she was made Iyalode or First Lady for her services against the Dahomey. She even interfered in politics there and helped to get her nominee Oyekan elected Alake in 1879. She was given a state funeral in Abeokuta when she died in 1887, and is commemorated in Lagos by the busy square named after her.

To the north the Fulani remained in Ilorin. At times Oyo alliances made attempts to dislodge them, for example when the Alafin Oluewe, Oluyole of Ibadan, Kurunmi of Ijaiye and the King of Bariba combined against Ilorin in the Eleduwe War. The Fulani proved too strong even for this combination. Oluewe was killed, Old Oyo was evacuated, and Oluewe's successor moved his capital to the present site Ago Oja.

The middle 1860s saw closer relations between Abeokuta and Lagos chiefly through the efforts of the British missionaries at Abeokuta. Each town had much to gain from co-operating commercially with the other, Abeokuta being the market where middlemen bought commodities such as cotton and kola nuts from the producers, and Lagos the market where the same middlemen sold them to the European merchants.

War in Western Nigeria was however not at an end. The efforts of Glover, the Governor of Lagos, to restrain the many rivalries were of little avail. In 1867 the Igbajo war broke out between Ibadan and Ijesha and seven Ijesha towns were sacked. The intervention of British officials from Lagos at Otta in Egba territory provoked a fresh quarrel with Abeokuta which resulted in the expulsion of British missionaries and Christian converts from Abeokuta and a campaign of persecution which ended the political influence of the missionaries there. Egba, Ijebu, Ijesha, Ilorin, Ibadan and Ekiti were in a state of general war, with Ibadan perhaps the most powerful force because of its more efficient government and because the rest of the area depended on it for protection against the ever-present Fulani threat.

It was Abeokuta that resisted the British threat longest. In 1892 a British expedition subdued Ijebu and in 1893 Bale (President) Fijabi of Ibadan accepted a British Resident. Abeokuta, however, would only accept a formal guarantee by the British of its independence and the setting-up in 1898 on British initiative of an Egba United Government; an experiment in democracy as interesting as that of the Province of Freedom in Sierra Leone. But the power of the Ologun or war-chiefs remained until the intervention of British troops in 1912. The Egba United Government was dissolved two years later.

In Ibadan towards the end of the century there was much internal unrest as well as external danger. At one time, in a war which ended in 1886, Ibadan found herself fighting Ilorin, Igbomina, Ijesha, Ekiti, the Egba, Ijebu and Ife. Captain Bower was the first Resident appointed under the 1893 agreement made between Bale Fijabi and the British, under which Ibadan was recognized as the administrative headquarters for a large area which included Iwo, Ede, Oshogbo, Ogbomosho, and Ikirun but remained subject to the overlordship of the Alafin of

Oyo, Emperor of the Yoruba. In 1897 an Executive Council was set up in Ibadan with the Resident as Chairman. In 1903 the Oja'ba Native Administration Court was established taking away some of the judicial powers of the kings and lords. In 1920 a Land Court and a Head Tax were introduced. In 1908 the link with Oyo was emphasized when Bale Sunmonu Apanpa went to Oyo for his inauguration; but interference with Ibadan's affairs by the Alafin was resented and after two Bales had been deposed for allowing such interference Okunola Basi assumed the title of Olubadan in 1936 and all traces of allegiance to Oyo disappeared.

LAGOS

The Lagos White Cap Chiefs are descendants of original settlers on the island and so traditionally hold rights over its lands. In the early eighteenth century King Akinsemoyin invited European slavers to do business with him and his subjects and so gave the history of Lagos its modern direction. One of the results of this invitation was that throughout the nineteenth century outsiders, African as well as European, interfered with and even controlled the politics of Lagos.

In 1819 Idewu Ojalari succeeded to the Lagos throne and ruled till 1832 when a former King, Adele, returned from exile in Badagry and regained the throne, probably with Egba help. He reigned only two years, and in 1834 was succeeded by Oluwole. Kosoko, son of Idewu Ojulari, soon conspired against Oluwole and was exiled to Porto Novo and Whydah. In 1841 Akitoye, Kosoko's uncle, succeeded to the throne and recalled his nephew from exile. He paid for this generosity in 1845. In that year Akitoye under pressure from the British abolished the slave trade. Two bitterly opposed factions appeared with Kosoko supporting that which favoured the continuation of the slave trade. After twelve days of civil war Kosoko emerged the winner, and Akitoye fled to Abeokuta.

Kosoko, King of Lagos

Kosoko became King of Lagos and his influence spread not only in Lagos but also in Abeokuta, with the result that Akitoye had to leave that city for Badagry. In Lagos the slave trade flourished again and Kosoko strengthened the defences against probable British intervention. Akitoye was forced to leave Badagry but this time was supported by the British Consul Beecroft whose headquarters were at Fernando Po. He championed Akitoye because he believed him genuinely opposed to the slave trade.

British intervene to restore Akitoye

Beecroft now called British arms to Akitoye's aid, and after an unsuccessful attempt captured Lagos in 1851 and restored Akitoye to his throne. Kosoko fled to Epe, and in January 1852 Akitoye signed a treaty with Britain abolishing slavery, guaranteeing Britain most-favoured-nation terms and allowing the entry of missionaries. A British vice-consul was appointed and the British West African Squadron which had effected the capture of Lagos was ready to intervene if Kosoko caused trouble; which he did unsuccessfully in 1852, Akitoye using Egba as well as British forces to crush the rising.

Dosunmu succeeds to the throne

In 1853 a new British consul, Benjamin Campbell, was appointed to Lagos while Beecroft acted as consul in the Bight of Biafra. In the same year Akitoye was succeeded by his son Dosunmu. Kosoko continued to cause annoyance by interfering with trade between Lagos and Abeokuta from his base at Epe, until in 1854 Campbell concluded an agreement with him by which he gave up his claims to Lagos in return for recognition as ruler of Palma and Lekki together with 2,000 heads of cowrie shells or 1,000 dollars a year for life. Kosoko also promised to give up slave trading and raiding Lagos's commerce. This agreement did not please the missionaries or Dosunmu or the Egba who feared Kosoko's friendship with the Dahomey. The missionaries themselves, especially Gollmer and Townsend, were out of favour with the merchants of Lagos, who resented their business activities and interference in politics, which Campbell attempted to check. It was at this time in 1856 that the British consul persuaded Dosunmu to expel the most successful of Lagos traders, Madame Tinubu (page 39). There were indeed many pretexts for British intervention in Lagos, especially as the population of the town was drawn from many Nigerian peoples including the 'emancipados' from Brazil and a large Bini community.

Lagos becomes a British Crown Colony, July 1861

In 1859 the war between Ibadan and Ijaiye (pp. 38-9) badly disrupted the trade of Lagos and so threatened the prosperity of the British merchants, who urged the British government to make Lagos a Crown Colony. They were opposed by the missionaries, who preferred things as they were. The merchants won, and on July 30, 1861 Dosunmu put his thumb-print to a treaty agreeing to the annexation of Lagos to the British Crown, on the terms put forward by Acting Consul McKoskry. These included a pension of over £1,000 a year for Dosunmu, whose agreement to the treaty was not obtained without difficulty, for he knew that by Lagos law and custom he could not alienate his land. The landing of British marines was timed to coincide with the treaty negotiations, and this forced his hand. The first Governor, Freeman, extended British territories, in spite of instructions to the contrary from the Colonial Office, annexing Palma, Lekki and Badagry, and destroying Epe. A pension was paid to Kosoko, whose territories were now included in the dependencies. In the same year, 1862, a Legislative Council was set up for this settlement and for sixty years it continued to advise the Governor. It always had an official majority and it was not until

1872 that an African, Captain J. P. L. Davies, was recommended by the Governor for appointment to the Council. By then, as a result of the recommendations of the Parliamentary Select Committee of 1865, Lagos was part of the West African Settlements under a Governor-in- Chief in Sierra Leone. The Lagos Legislative Council still continued to function, but it advised an Administrator in Lagos who was responsible to the Governor-in-Chief. Between 1874 and 1886, indeed, Lagos was regarded as part of the Gold Coast Colony. Nevertheless the British made it the base from which they extended their control over the whole of Yorubaland. By 1893 most of what is now Western Nigeria was in practice a British Protectorate attached to the Colony of Lagos. British control became complete in 1914.

With the Legislative Council being so completely a 'closed shop' - when it was dissolved in 1922 it still only included two Africans - interest in Lagos politics tended to be centred on the Lagos Town Council whose members were first elected, as distinct from being appointed, in 1920. This led to the creation of political parties in the town, and in 1923 Herbert Macaulay's Nigerian National Democratic Party, perhaps the first truly nationalist party in Nigeria, was formed. It was supported by the Lagos Market Women's Guild amongst others, and until the emergence of the Nigerian Youth Movement in 1936 regularly won the triennial municipal elections. Although at first the N.N.D.P. was almost entirely limited to Lagos, it later showed its interest in wider spheres by joining the National Congress of British West Africa and the National Council of Nigeria and the Cameroons (now the National Congress of Nigerian Citizens). In 1964 the name Nigerian National Democratic Party was revived by Chief Akintola for his party in the West.

THE MID-WEST

The people of Benin are mainly Edo-speaking. Their King, the Oba, was as far back as the fifteenth century subject in spiritual matters to the Oni of Ife and until the nineteenth century in political matters to the Alafin of Oyo. Benin itself made its own very important contributions to the life and wealth of this part of Nigeria. Benin bronzes are now world-famous and a description of the method of making them has been given in Volume One of this history. It was, however, Benin's pepper that brought her to the notice of Europe, for in 1485 the Portuguese sailor João Affonso D'Aveiro took samples of this pepper home together with the King of Gwato, Benin's port. This alternative source of this spice was much valued and Portugal established a trading post at Gwato in 1486. In 1553 the English sailor Captain Windham took three ships to the Benin River, visited the Oba, and was offered eighty tons of pepper on credit, the Portuguese having ceased trading in African pepper in favour of East Indian supplies of the commodity.

Settlers from Benin went to various parts of Nigeria, e.g. Bini to Lagos (page 42) and Itsekiri down the Benin River and to Warri which was settled by Prince Ginuwa, son of Oba Olua. Those who settled along the banks of the Benin River were first noticed by Europeans at Eghoro opposite the mouth of the creek leading to Gwato. The Itsekiri were traders in cloth, gin, guns, palm products, fish and salt. Another people who may have originated in Benin are the Ijaw. Brass too may have been founded from Benin on the Nun River which with the Forcados River is the true estuary of the Niger.

It must be said that we do not know a great deal of the history of Benin itself before the nineteenth century. It was during this century that the Oba threw off allegiance to the Alafin of Oyo. Though the Oba was nominally sovereign he was as much under the influence of his priests in the same way as the Alake of Abeokuta was dominated by the Ologun. Benin's commercial relations with Europeans grew stronger, especially after two English firms anchored their ships near the Benin River in the 1840s, and in the following decade built factories (or trading warehouses) along its banks.

The Itsekiri migration to the Benin River was brought about by the death in 1848 of the Itsekiri King Akengbuwa and his two sons. In the confusion that followed two separate streams of Itsekiri refugees moved out of Benin; one with the remnants of the royal family settled on the south bank of the Benin River, the other led by the Ologbotsere family under Idobofun on the north bank. These settlements not only quarrelled among themselves but had to fight off attacks from the Ijaw. They also had to endure interference from the British Consul, Beecroft, who favouring the non-royalist section appointed Diare, brother of Idobofun, 'governor' of the Benin River. On Diare's death in 1870, the British appointed Chanowi, a member of the royal family of the south bank community, to succeed him; and, when he failed to serve their interests satisfactorily, again looked to the north bank for the next 'governor'. This was Olomu, the founder of Ebrohimi, a man of wealth and influence who was able to restore peace to the Benin River; which suited the British so well that they appointed his son, Nanna, to succeed him.

Nanna, Governor of the Benin River

Having had a British appointed 'governor' for thirty years, the Itsekiri had come to accept his authority. Nanna at the same time acknowledged his allegiance to the Oba of Benin. Nanna, a natural leader of ability, promoted peaceful commerce and sternly suppressed war among the Itsekiri or with the Ijaw or other neighbours, and put down piracy by the Ijaw and Urhobo. Increased trade led to improved design in trading canoes, and improved buildings, especially improved roofing tiles. So successful was Nanna that it was said he, at one stage, had 20,000 people working for him.

A weakness in Nanna's position was the fact that he was appointed by the British. In 1884 he accepted British protection and in 1889 formally recognized that this protection came from the British Queen and not from the trading companies. He was therefore dependent on the British for the continuance of this authority. A rift came in 1894. In 1891 the British sent a Vice Consul, Gallwey, to the Benin River, and he in fact took over most of Nanna's duties as 'governor'. Sensing that Nanna was losing favour with his patrons, his many enemies began to press charges against him. The royalists scorned him as a commoner; European traders charged him with preventing them from opening factories at Sapele and Benin City; missionaries accused him of engaging in the local slave trade, and indeed of owning slaves who terrorized the neighbourhood. The acting British Consul-General, Ralph Moor, called Nanna to Lagos to answer the charges. Nanna, however, refused to leave his chief town Ebrohimi. He even stood firm when the first warship was sent, but left for Lagos when a whole fleet began to maneuvre to attack his town. The British entered Ebrohimi where they seized £3,000 worth of cloth and nearly 8,000 cases of gin. Nanna was tried in Calabar, and exiled first to Cross River and then to Accra.

The Oba Overami of Benin — the fall of Benin

The lesson of the fate of Nanna was not lost on his acknowledged overlord, the Oba Overami of Benin. He ruled at the end of the nineteenth century over territory bounded by the River Bonny, Lagos and Idah, but his political power except in Benin was in serious decline. Even in Benin he was, like many West African rulers elsewhere, mainly a ceremonial and spiritual figure heavily dependent in political and judicial matters on the priests who surrounded him. In 1892 Overami agreed to abolish slavery. This agreement had no force, and in 1895 Overami, seeing what had happened to Nanna, decided to exclude all foreigners. The Acting Consul-General, Phillips, decided in 1896 to press for adherence to the agreement and also claimed that Overami had accepted British protection. Early in 1897 he set out for Benin at the time of the great Agne festival when the Oba could see no man but a Bini. It was also a time when there were human sacrifices. Phillips did not heed a request for a postponement of his visit for two months, partly because he feared the extension of French power in the region. In a consequent dispute Phillips and five others of the British party of nine were killed, probably at the instigation of Ologbosere, one of Oba's subject chiefs. The remainder of the party escaped and brought the news back to Lagos. Six weeks later a naval expedition entered Benin and terrorized the city with its rockets. The attack may have led to further human sacrifices before the city fell. The Oba fled but six months later was surrendered. He was tried and with his three wives deported to Calabar where he died and was buried in 1914. His son succeeded him as Oba. By their conquest the British opened up 3,000 square miles producing valuable rubber and palm products. They also took 2,500 of the magnificent Benin bronzes which were sent back to Europe.

Nanna the Itsekiri was treated more favourably than Overami. He was succeeded as leader of his people by Dore Nume, but was allowed to return from Accra in 1906 and to found a new town near Koko, where he died in 1916.

THE EAST

Whilst the history of those parts of Nigeria so far described in this volume is dominated by the activities and rivalries of hereditary rulers, and their relationships with the British, the history to be told in this chapter is that of a number of states whose leaders owed their position to ability, not birth.

Bonny

Bonny is one of the most important of these states. Originally an Ijaw fishing village, it became during the nineteenth century the leading Delta state in the palm-oil trade, as in the previous century it had led in the slave trade. Its population by this time was largely Ibo and Ibibio, but still numbered fewer than 10,000. Its ruler could only win and maintain his position by gaining a considerable share in a market where in the early years of the century there was fierce competition in the trade in which both slaves and palm-oil were offered in exchange for commodities manufactured in Europe.

The kings of Bonny were very jealous of the power they had struggled to gain. When in 1824 the British Captain W. F. W. Owen surveyed the coasts without King Opubu Pepple's permission, he reminded the British of his sovereignty by forbidding his subjects to trade with them. This king is known to history as Opubu the Great. He was of Ibo descent and the third member of his family to wear the Bonny crown. The monarchy was probably established as early as the fifteenth century. Opubu, the fourteenth king of Bonny, had begun his reign in 1792. He not only sought to protect his sovereignty against Britain, but also to extend it by attacking Calabar. In this he failed. He died in 1830, leaving as his heir William Dappa Pepple, who was a minor. For the next five years two Regents ruled Bonny, first an ex-slave, Madu, till 1833, and then his eldest son Alali until 1835. William, when he came of age in 1835, found Alali well entrenched in power, and he had to wait for an opportunity to dislodge him. This came in 1837 when the British Navy, in accordance with the terms of the Equipment Treaty, seized two Portuguese slave-ships in the port of Bonny. Alali, perhaps to show his desire to protect Bonny waters, imprisoned three British naval officers and thereby provoked British action against the port. William at once allied with the British and with their help got rid of Alali. He had no intention, however, of being subservient to the British and always had Bonny's interests in mind. He signed an agreement with the British to cease trading in slaves and to develop the trade in palm-oil. As a result, in the following ten years the oil trade of Bonny doubled; the King himself probably made between £15,000 and £20,000 from it.

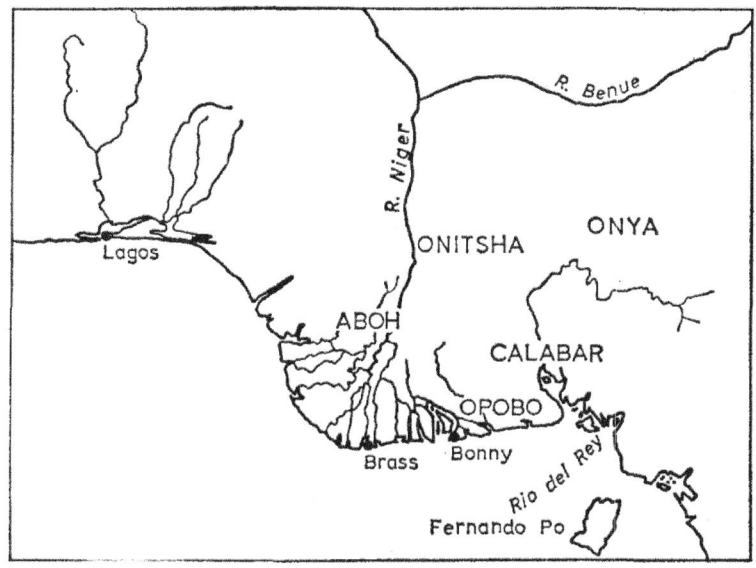

MAP 3 THE EAST AND THE DELTA
(Creek Town, Henshaw Town and Duke Town are suburbs of the modern town of Calabar.)

He used a fleet of large war canoes powerfully armed and manned which penetrated the farthest corners of the Delta creeks. He thus earned £500,000 worth of trade a year for his state, much of it from Ibo and Ibibio country.

Of course William Pepple had his enemies, internal and external. Fighting between Bonny and Calabar continued without decisive result. Internally he bought or frightened off those who might have challenged his position, and ruled very much as he wished. It is a tribute to him that he used his power wisely. One enemy was biding his time, the former Regent Alali. As long as the interests of Bonny and Britain could be served by the same policy, all went well for William. But between 1847 and 1850 he found it more profitable to trade with other European competitors than with British merchants, and finally stopped trade with the British altogether. The British Consul Beecroft would not tolerate this, and finding a ready ally in Alali he struck in 1854 when William fell ill and there was a dispute about a Regent. Beecroft deposed William who was sent into exile successively to Fernando Po, Ascension and London, a puppet, Dappo, being installed in his stead. Dappo, however, died in 1855, and Bonny was plunged into a series of civil wars which persisted until 1875 and spread to other city states in the Delta. In Bonny the wars were started by ex-slaves, who often showed themselves resourceful and resilient. William Dappa Pepple, much westernized after his exile in London, was restored in 1861, and was succeeded on his death by his English-educated son, George, who was controlled by the British. The trade of Bonny during this period was stimulated in the early 1850s by the founding of the African Steamship Company by Macgregor Laird. This company, which later became Elder Dempster, enabled the individual trader, African and European, to get his goods to market without having first to sell them to the European firms who owned ships. In the late 1850s, however, the trade of Bonny was threatened when Macgregor Laird established factories at Aboh, Onitsha and Lokoja between 1857 and 1859.

Opobo

A notable figure in the sixties was Jaja who was bought in an Ibo slave market in 1860 and who quickly rose through his ability from slavery to leadership. There were six 'houses' in Bonny each with its own head, Annie Pepple, Captain Hart, Adda Allison, Manilla Pepple, Oko Jumbo and Jim Bango; these were trading, social and political organizations and it was in the house of Annie Pepple that Jaja rose to power in 1869. In 1870 he lost a struggle against the rival house of Oko Jumbo, and left Bonny to found a new trading state in Opobo, which in time became more important than Bonny. He was recognized as King of Opobo not only by Britain but also by other European powers who were looking for allies and later for 'spheres of influence'. Jaja even sent a contingent to assist the British in the Asante War. He was not, however, subservient to the British and when he annexed Qua Eboe, which was inland from Opobo, he declared it a market for Opobo traders only and banned the British from it. He hoped to give Opobo traders the monopoly of the important oil-producing centre, the Esene, which lay in the Opobo hinterland.

Jaja refused to give way to British pressure and change his policy, though he accepted British protection in 1885 when the 'Scramble for Africa' began. He insisted on an explanation of 'protection'; and was assured by Consul Hewett that it did not mean annexation, that his markets were safe, and that free trade was not insisted on. There were later disputes with Hewett who unsuccessfully attempted to impose a fine on Jaja for breaking the treaty. In 1887 Hewett was relieved by an Acting Consul, Harry Johnston, who afterwards gained fame in East Africa. Johnston was much more ruthless in his action against Jaja whom he described as 'the most grasping, unscrupulous and overbearing of mushroom kings'. In Johnston's opinion the monopoly of Opobo had to be broken if British commercial interests in the Delta were to advance. He, therefore, declared Jaja had broken the treaty of protection, although one British firm, Miller Brothers, supported the King. Johnston lured Jaja on to a British boat and virtually kidnapped him, later explaining that his action was the result of an ambiguous cable from the Foreign Office. Jaja, who had put up a stout fight for the rights of African kings, was deported first to the Gold Coast and later to the West Indies. He repeatedly demanded his return, and in 1889 the British Government, finding that Opobo needed Jaja, agreed to the recommendation of the Special Commissioner, Major Claude MacDonald, that he should be allowed to return. Unfortunately he died on his way home in 1891. He was buried in Opobo.

Other Delta states

There were many other states in the Delta in the nineteenth century — most of them ports used by European merchants. Brief mention has been made of Aboh, Bonny's former market and later rival, which under her King Obi Ossai became important in war as well as in trade in the middle of the century. Like Assay, Uchi, Onya and Onitsha, Aboh was probably founded by the Ibo-speaking Ika people in the middle of the seventeenth century. Unlike the Ibo the Ika had royal houses. Other settlements on the Niger were made by Ibo and Igala people from the east and by fugitives from the Fulani from the north. Thus the Delta was a melting pot of people, Bini, Ijaw, Sobo, Itsekiri, Ekoi, Ibibio, Ika, Efik and others, including people from the north. To the Ibo, the Delta-dwellers are 'People of the Salt Water', dependent on the sea and seafarers for their livelihood. To the Europeans in the nineteenth century they were proud and independent — Jaja was typical of them — and forced the British to do business with them from ships anchored off shore, discharging their cargoes into barracoons, and not from factories and forts as elsewhere in West Africa.

These Delta states had no common forms of government. In Bonny the King's powers were limited; he had to accept the advice of the Council. Jaja was a self-made autocrat. Old Calabar, on the other hand, was a federation of republics, such as Creek Town, Henshaw Town, Duke Town and Obutong. Originally Ijaw fishing villages, these Old Calabar states were developed and settled by Efik people between the fifteenth and the eighteenth centuries. The Egbo secret society was very powerful in Old Calabar, and regulated the political, economic and social affairs of each state. Each state, like Jaja's Opobo, had a hinterland which it regarded as its special preserve and from which commerce flowed exclusively to it. This hinterland it jealously guarded against intruders, African or European.

On page 44 the origin of Brass, another of these city states, has been mentioned. In the nineteenth century Brass became the centre of slave smuggling on a very large scale, with Onitsha as its chief market. The Aro are a section of the Ibo people who won a special position of authority and commercial importance in the east, in theory because of the divinely given Aro Chuku Oracle, but also because they had twenty-five carefully sited settlements along key trade routes. Their power was widely feared during the era of the slave trade, and they exploited this fear to their commercial advantage. The majority of Ibo people still today look to Nri in Awka as their spiritual home and to the Eze as their spiritual leader, as the Yoruba looked to the Oni. The Ibo were much less in touch with European missionaries and traders than the people of the West in this century, and this, combined with the lack of royal houses and records, has made their history more difficult to trace than that of the West and Mid-West.

Growth of British interest

In the nineteenth century Britain first used Fernando Po as her base from which to watch over and promote her interests in the Bight of Biafra, where French, Spanish and Portuguese were also active. Fernando Po was leased for a time from Spain on the suggestion of Captain Owen, who was made superintendent. He endeavoured to get the Court of Mixed Commission transferred there in 1830; had he succeeded many Yoruba slaves would have been freed nearer home and the history of modern Sierra Leone would have been very different. The Spanish appointed Beecroft Governor of Fernando Po in 1843 and the Baptists established a mission there, but in 1858 the Spanish Government took over active control.

Britain's interest in the Niger area was shown in exploration as well as in missionary and commercial activity. After the Lander brothers had traced out the mouth of the Niger in 1830, a bitter feud started between old established traders and African middlemen on the one hand and explorers and abolitionists on the other, as to whether European traders should continue their old methods of trade or sail their ships up the great river and deal direct with the palm-oil producers of the hinterland. Men like the Landers, Macgregor Laird, Beecroft, Barth, Caillie and Dr Baikie played their part in the exploration and opening up of the Niger and Benue rivers. The British Government was, at this time, anxious to leave the African states their trade if they would give up slaving. Indeed they found it difficult to get the rulers of the city states to sign anti-slave trade treaties. Furthermore Britain was reluctant to incur any more expense by extending her authority, though her representatives such as Beecroft often presented London with a *fait accompli*. We have seen examples of this interference in Bonny and Opobo; a further example was when on the death of King Archibong of Calabar in 1852, Beecroft presided over the election of a successor. As a result of such interference civil war spread, between the middle of the century and 1875 (page 47), to New Calabar or Kalabiri where two houses, Barboy and Amakiri, struggled for power. In Old Calabar the British had destroyed the authority of the people who used to keep law and order in the area. The Egbo secret society was attacked, not always openly, by British missionary societies like the Scottish Presbyterian Mission which arrived in Duke Town and Creek Town in 1846 and in Bonny in 1864. It was not surprising then that the civil fighting in Old Calabar took the form of a series of bloody revolts of domestic slaves against the Egbo

Nigeria in the Nineteenth Century

secret society, quelled with British help. And in New Calabar, the Amakiri house had by 1873 emerged the victor.

In the 1860s, with the slave trade suppressed and the oil trade moving inland up the Niger to Laird's new factories, Bonny, Brass, Old Calabar and Opobo were doomed commercially. The first two fought back gamely for a while to prevent British steamers reaching Onitsha and Aboh. But war canoes were no match for the frigates which Laird had now persuaded the British Government to use to protect this greatly enriched trade.

It was this same prosperity which made it inevitable that in spite of the checks which the Report of the Parliamentary Select Committee of 1865 caused in the extension of British rule in Nigeria and elsewhere in West Africa, the pressure of local officials and merchants for annexation should continue. Every year Britain became more and more interested in what had now come to be known as the Oil Rivers of Nigeria. A Court of Equity was set up in Bonny to judge disputes between Europeans and Africans. After 1870 London and other British ports joined Liverpool in drawing great wealth from the area. In 1872 the British consulate was transferred from Fernando Po to Old Calabar. Six years later £309,200 worth of trade was carried by fourteen steamers operated between the Niger and Britain by four large British firms. In 1879 Sir George Goldie merged these and other firms into the United Africa Company, which in the following year was to be found trading 600 miles up the Niger.

The pressure on the British government to declare a protectorate in the area was irresistible; but what the government was being pressed to do was to protect British investments rather than Nigerian peoples. The French and Germans would very soon annex what the British did not.

On May the 16th, 1884, Consul Hewitt was given by his government the authority by which he sought and obtained Jaja's signature to a treaty of 'protection'. Between July and September he collected the other necessary signatures. On June the 5th, 1885 a British Protectorate was formally declared over the Niger districts lying between Lagos, Rio del Rey, the Benue and the sea. It was just in time, for 1885 was the year of the Berlin Conference and the start of the European 'Scramble for Africa'. Britain had been forced by international circumstances to repudiate the Select Committee Report of 1865.

THE NORTH

In Volume One of this history, brief mention was made of Usman dan Fodio and the Fulani Jihad which transformed the political structure of Northern Nigeria and the influence of which is still strongly felt today. At the end of the eighteenth

West Africa in History

century no one could have foreseen the impact which this elderly and learned teacher and this people would have on the Hausa kingdoms of the North.

The Fulani, a race of cattle nomads, began to enter what is now Northern Nigeria in the thirteenth century. Some of them were light-skinned and their origin is still a matter for research, but it is believed that they came from Fouta Jallon. By the sixteenth century they had spread throughout the Western Sudan, from Senegal to the Cameroons. We learn that they made a successful attack on Bornu in 1660; that in 1700 they sacked the great city of Kano, and that well before 1800 they were attacking the Jukun in the Benue area. They remained mostly nomadic cattle-owners but there were some, the Fulani Gidda, who became town-dwellers. The latter were strict Moslems and among them were many scholars and intellectuals who attacked the religious slackness of the Hausa states. Among these scholars was Usman dan Fodio who came from the Fulani clan of Fouta Toro which had migrated fourteen generations before and settled in Gobir. Usman was born in 1744 and his brother, Abdullahi, in 1756. He was brought up in a village called Degel, and he returned there to teach the Muslim religion after completing his traditional Islamic studies at Agades.

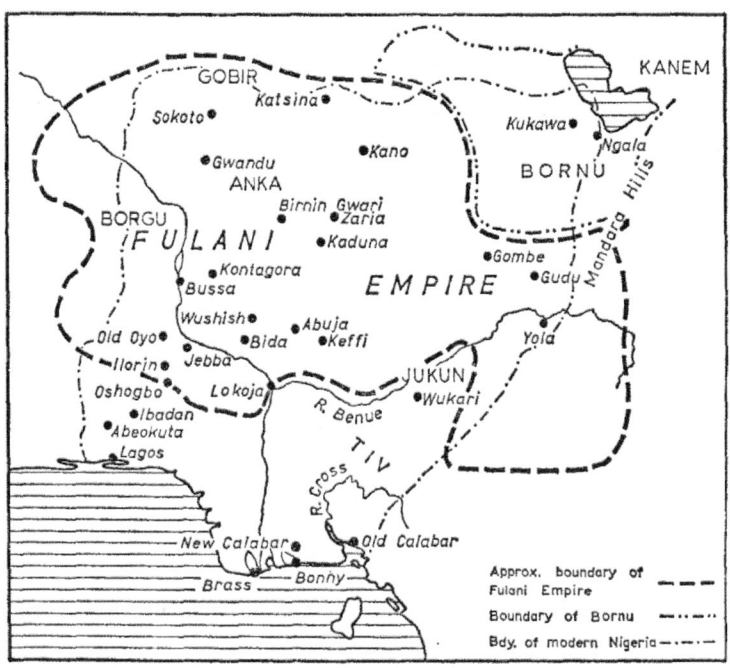

MAP 4 THE FULANI EMPIRE

Soon his reputation as a scholar and teacher reached Alkalawa, the capital of the King of Gobir; and Usman was appointed tutor of the children of the King, Nafata. The latter nominally accepted Islam, but like most of the Habe rulers of

Hausaland he intermingled idolatry and Habe paganism with Muslim rites. Usman soon fell out with Yunfa, who had been his pupil, and who succeeded to the throne in 1802. The Shehu, as he is called, retired to Degel where he attracted many pupils and to which Yunfa pursued him, seeing in his puritanical reforms a threat to the royal power. Usman was forced to flee from Degel to Gudu where his brother, Abdullahi, made a call to arms. Usman was elected leader of the revolt and his followers did homage to him as the Sheikh at the head of the Jihad or Holy War. Round him Hausa and Fulani alike rallied, some in protest against the King's attack on their teacher, some in defence of the true Faith against the attacks made on Islam by Yunfa, and yet others because of personal grievances against the Gobir King. Usman was proclaimed Sarkin Musulmi in 1804 and, urged by his followers, attacked and put to flight the Gobirawa, the forces of Yunfa, capturing Gobir and its subject towns. Leaving the direction of the war to his brother Abdullahi and his son Muhammed Bello, Usman, in the traditional Muslim fashion, gave flags to his commanders urging them to set forth to defend the Faith wherever they found it to be in danger.

The Jihad spread like a bush fire. The Fulani had in their strong cavalry a great advantage over their enemies, and their leaders knew not only that success would be a service to the Prophet, but that conquest under one of Usman's flags would win them an emirate. For the next six years warfare was incessant, and at times the success of the Jihad was in the balance. Usman's base camp was at Sabougari to the north of the Zamfara capital of Anka. There he received his leaders, and thence he sent them out with his blessing. In 1806 the formidable Tuareg army was defeated by the Fulani, and although Borgu and Bornu (thanks to El Kanemi) and isolated places such as Oshogbo to the south of Ilorin held out, it was clear by 1809 that Usman had won the north. In 1807 he entered Kano in triumph. Katsina, Zaria and Sokoto successively opened their gates to him, and to the last named town he retired in 1809. By 1811 his empire extended over a hundred thousand square miles in provinces ruled by his flag-bearers as Emirs. He handed on his political power to his brother, Abdullahi, at Gwandu, and his son, Muhammed Bello, at Sokoto. Usman in the latter years contented himself with acting as elder statesman and spiritual father and building the city wall of Sokoto where he died in 1817.

At the time of Usman's death the Fulani controlled a vast area extending from Borgu in the west to the Mandara Hills in the east, and from the desert in the north to the Yoruba town of Oshogbo in the south. There remained some independent areas like Bornu within this domain. There was no single government administering the Fulani Empire, but rather scores of separate states each ruled over originally by a flag-bearer selected by Usman dan Fodio. Early on there was some friction between Abdullahi at Gwandu and Muhammed Bello at Sokoto before the supremacy of the latter was recognized. Today the Sardauna of Sokoto, a direct descendant of the Shehu, remains predominant among the traditional rulers of Northern Nigeria.

When the territory of the empire founded by Usman was occupied by the British in 1900—3 its structure remained as it was in 1811 and most of the Emirs were descended from Usman's flag-bearers. Usman's success was partly the result of his single-minded devotion to his faith and partly to the support he received from Hausa as well as Fulani.

Bornu

In the far north of Nigeria lies its largest province, Bornu, a country whose history is better known than that of some more accessible parts because of the care with which its inhabitants. the Kanuri, have preserved its records. The people of Bornu by the beginning of the nineteenth century were under a weak government. They were descended from the Sefuwa or Maighumi people who were of Tuareg blood and had come from the desert before the end of the first century A.D., settling eventually in Kanem, east of Lake Chad. When other desert peoples attacked Kanem, descendants of the early settlers moved west of the lake to Bornu.

The Bornu people reached their greatest strength under the distinguished Mais (or rulers) of the Maighumi royal house in the sixteenth century. In the course of time the Mais, though remaining good Moslems (unlike the Kings of Hausaland), became weaker and their country became the prey of the desert Tuaregs who frequently overran its frontiers. They soon found enemies also within the frontiers. There were Fulani in Bornu as well as in the Hausa states; and the 1804 Fulani Jihad in Hausaland was echoed in Bornu, and for a time it seemed that Bornu would fall under Fulani domination. The capital of the Mai Ahmad, Gasreggemo, fell to the Fulani in 1808. It seemed that all was lost when a saviour arose. Sheikh Muhammed El Amin El Kanemi was born in the Fezzan, of Kanem parents, about thirty years before the Jihad. He performed the pilgrimage as a young man and married the daughter of the governor of a Bornu province whose capital was at Ngala, south-west of the Lake. When the Fulani attacked, he gathered some of his fellow Kanembu, who were better fighters than the Bornu, and defended his father-in-law's territory.

El Kanemi as he came to be called had already established a reputation for his learning and goodness. Like Usman, he took the title of Shehu and enforced a strict observance of the tenets of the Muslim faith. El Kanemi, having repelled the Fulani attack on Ngala, turned to help the Mai Ahmad, whom he restored. After Ahmad's death in 1810 El Kanemi went to the assistance of his successor Dunama, and their united forces drove the Fulani armies out of the Bornu capital. El Kanemi now not only enjoyed great wealth but also the devotion of the masses. The ungrateful Dunama, jealous of El Kanemi's success, plotted to have him removed from the kingdom. Most men in El Kanemi's position would have regarded this as sufficient reason to seize for themselves the throne they had saved. El Kanemi merely placed a more prudent member of Dunama's family on the throne and contented himself by exercising the real power. For himself he took only the title 'Servant of God'.

He devoted the rest of his life to advising the king as to how to restore law and order and recover some of Bornu's former prosperity, leading its defence against the Fulani to the west and the Baghirmi to the south, re-establishing suzereignty over Kanem and building a new city at Kukawa in which to retire. He would not allow the king to enter into treaties with Europeans under which traders, missionaries or explorers would have to be freely admitted; for he sensed the danger to the kingdom which such an influx of foreigners would raise. But in 1823 he was visited by Major Denham, the British explorer, who admired his intelligence and kindliness, and lived in Bornu for over a year. He recognized El Kanemi as the real ruler of Bornu, and left us an excellent picture of that country's saviour. El Kanemi died in 1835; and ten years later the last Mai King was deposed by Sheikh Umar, El Kanemi's eldest son. A descendant of El Kanemi is the ruler of Bornu today.

The Jukun

The Jukun were originally a Hamitic people, probably from Kordofan. Their Empire at various times stretched north to Bornu (where they once had their capital), south to the Cross River, west to the Niger, and east to the twelfth meridian. Unlike Bornu it was conquered in the early years of the nineteenth century by the Fulani, under the leadership of Buba Yero, who was assisted by Yakuba, first Emir of Bauchi; and Buba Yero's grandson Koiranga echoed this triumph by taking the Jukun town of Pindiga about sixty years later. Under frequent attack from the Fulani, the Jukun kings were put on the defensive throughout the century. In about 1840 we learn of King Kakanja's building a new capital at the present Wukari. In the 1860s during the reign of King Agbumanu the Jukun had been compelled by Fulani attacks to cease their ancient practice of raiding their neighbours the Tiv for slaves, and to negotiate for Tiv help in the defence of Wukari. But the alliance was short-lived, and by the beginning of the present century Tiv and Jukun were once more at daggers drawn. For a few years, with the assistance of the Emir of Muri, the Jukun King Agudu Manu subdued the Tiv, but a professional soldier called Dankoro freed them. The Jukun, like the Bibi and the Aro, had a religious and cultural influence farther reaching and longer lasting than their political or military domination. For example their belief in the divinity of their kings is shared by many of their neighbours.

Kontagora

Right across on the other side of Northern Nigeria to the west lies the emirate of Kontagora. Here too the role of the Fulani was very important. The town was founded by a Fulani leader Umoru who was a grandson of dan Fodio and who lived from 1806 to 1876. He took the title of Nagwamatse of Kontagora which he founded in 1863 and made his capital. His brother Ahmadu was Sultan of Sokoto from 1859 onwards and Umoru acknowledged Ahmadu as his overlord in return for having the additional title 'Zarikin Sudan' or 'Lord of the Blacks' conferred on him. Umoru was utterly ruthless, butchering and enslaving the peoples in his path. Much of his emirate remains to this day very sparsely populated as a consequence of his excesses. Umoru's titles were passed on to Mobido, his son, in 1876, then to Ibrahim, Mobido's son, in 1880. Of these rulers Ibrahim proved the most successful in adding to the power of the state of Kontagora. He extended its frontiers until it stretched as far as Birnin Gwari and touched the Emir of Yauri's territory. Ibrahim was also a determined slave raider, and this was to lead to his downfall. For by the end of the century the British had established a post at Wushishi on the Kaduna River and within his territory; and after the Asante War seasoned West African Frontier Force troops had little difficulty in taking the Nagwamatse's capital (1901), as part of the general British advance into Northern Nigeria at the time. Ibrahim fled to Kaya in the Zaria emirate. The British followed and arrested him, took him to Lokoja and then to Yola. However, unable to find an effective substitute, the British restored him in 1903. He died in 1922.

Conclusion

In so vast an area as that affected by the Fulani Jihad it has been possible to mention only a few states. So far little has been said about the Fulani in the south. Here these people experienced greater difficulties than those in the North, as they were faced by Nupe and Yorubaland. In Nupe with the aid of Mallam Dendo they obtained an insecure foothold. In Yorubaland they established themselves in Ilorin chiefly through the agency of Mallam Alimi who supported the Kakanfo Afonja's revolt against Oyo, but who like El Kanemi did not depose the existing ruler. In 1831, however, Afonja was killed by Alimi's son who reigned in his stead as first Fulani Emir of Ilorin.

As has been stated earlier, the Fulani Empire, organized on the lines laid down by Usman dan Fodio, remained in being until the British took over the country. It not only gave a uniform pattern of government but stimulated commerce and brought comparative peace to an area long torn by war. Though decay set in in many parts, some areas like Sokoto remained distinguished for just and good administration.

3

Sovereignty Regained: The Gambia, Sierra Leone, Ghana

As late as 1951 an Englishman, F. J. Pedler, wrote (in a book entitled *West Africa*):

'Even if Nigeria and the Gold Coast can be visualized as self-governing units in the comity of nations (and this assumes that the Gold Coast will not suffer eclipse from the cocoa disease), Sierra Leone and the Gambia can hardly aspire to such a status.'

Yet ten years later all but the Gambia had achieved independence, and the Gambia was approaching it. In this chapter we shall study the origins and course of this West African revolution. We are too close to it to see it clearly. The historian's eyes demand distance in order to focus accurately. So all we can do at present is to sketch in barest outline the course of events so far as we can make it out today.

a. THE GAMBIA

The defeat of Fodi Kabba by the British in 1892 and declaration of the Gambia Protectorate two years later did not end opposition to the British presence in the Gambia. In 1900 the Marabout of Sankandi killed the members of a British expedition which was trying to make peace between them and their old enemies the Soninke, in a relatively small quarrel over a rice field. Fodi Kabba began to rebuild his strength whilst the British recovered from the blow. As soon as they had done so, they decided he must be crushed once and for all.

Fortunately for the British the risings in Sierra Leone and the South African and Asante wars had all now ended, and it was possible to assemble a substantial force in the Gambia. As had been done with King Dosunmu of Lagos, bribery was used to secure the co-operation of the Fulani king, Musa Molloh of Faladu: he was given a stipend of £500 per annum in return for agreeing to help the British and to place Faladu under their protection. The British also secured the support of the French who, having finally defeated Samori in 1898, after half a century of fighting, wanted to see the end of this other obstinately anti-European

African. Fodi Kabba stood no chance against such a combination: in 1901 Medina, his stockaded headquarters, fell.

The British had one final African enemy to crush. King Wappai of Foni gave shelter to a man accused of committing murder in another kingdom. The British ordered him to give up the accused. He refused. The British moved towards his capital with the new West African Frontier Force, and King Wappai fled in terror (1904).

Ten years later peace in West Africa was to be shattered by a world war starting in Europe. Trade was completely disrupted; but Britain who gained most from her trade with the Gambia also suffered most from the dislocation of trade. The Gambian soldiers played their part well in a conflict they did not understand, from which they had nothing to gain or lose, and which was to prove incomparably more wasteful of human life than any wars in which Africans had previously been engaged. Above all, it was to prove completely futile; for all the things fought for in 1914—18 had to be fought for again, at even greater cost, twenty years after the peace.

However, Gambians went to the Cameroons in 1915 and to East Africa in 1917 and fought gallantly. They did the same in Burma in the Second World War (1939—45). But during these campaigns they learnt more than merely how to fight: they travelled to, or through, non-European countries which were either independent or struggling to become so. Seeds were planted in receptive West African minds.

In the economic and social fields the colony's progress was still slow. In 1902 the total public revenue was only £50,000, most of it obtained from export duties on groundnuts. With the discovery of *Trypanosoma gambiense*[1] by the Principal Medical Officer of the Gambia, Dr R. M. Forde, in 1901, it was realized that economic, social and scientific co-operation between the various colonies of West Africa might be to the advantage of all. In 1902 the West African Medical Service was set up. It was to be followed during the next fifty years by many other similar bodies, including the West African War Council (which controlled the West African Frontier Force), the West African Currency Board, the West African Rice, Cocoa, Fisheries and Oil Palm Research Institutes, the West African Institute for Social and Economic Research, the West African Examinations Council and West African Airways. These inter-territorial bodies, however, were not designed to meet the needs of fully independent nations.

---

[1] *Trypanosoma gambiense* is the organism which causes sleeping sickness in man. Other similar organisms cause disease in cattle, horses and other domesticated animals. All these organisms are carried by tsetse flies throughout West Africa.

Sovereignty Regained: The Gambia, Sierra Leone, Ghana

When the countries supporting them gained independence, these associations were broken up. The West African Examinations Council alone survives today.

Progress was also made in the Gambia with the stamping out of the social evils of slavery and slave trading. Forbidden for a century to British subjects, both practices were still legally permitted to Gambians in the Protectorate, who were 'protected persons'. In 1906 a second Slave Trade Abolition Ordinance was enacted, and in 1930 an Abolition of Slavery Ordinance.

Political progress was equally slow. In 1935 the Governor's Executive and Legislative Councils still consisted entirely of members nominated by the Governor, and of British officials. In 1946 the Bathurst Town Council was founded; and the growing political consciousness which the Second World War had brought throughout West Africa led to this council being given a majority of elected members. However, the British kept a careful control of its activities by appointing the administrative officer who was Commissioner of the Colony as president of this council.

During the following years another step forward in the development of democratic local government was taken when the Kombo Rural Authority was created and given responsibility for Kombo St Mary. Its members were nominated by the Governor from amongst the headmen of the villages near Bathurst; but again the Colony Commissioner was made president. In the Protectorate four divisions were created: the Western, Central, MacCarthy Island and Upper River. Each of these was subdivided into a number of districts. Each of these districts had its own native authorities, consisting of kings and their advisers. And again, like Bathurst and Kombo St Mary, each protectorate division had a British Commissioner keeping vigilant watch over its administration. Justice was dispensed by a Supreme Court, subordinate to which were a civil Court of Requests and a police court in Bathurst, and native courts in the Protectorate.

Then in 1947 the first advance towards democracy at the central government level was made when the Legislative Council was given two elected members, who represented Bathurst and Kombo St Mary. Four years later it had eight unofficial members, two elected to represent Bathurst, one Kombo St Mary, one each of the four protectorate divisions and one nominated to represent commercial interests. This council was usually presided over, not as previously by the Governor, but by a Vice-President, who was a Gambian. The Executive Council was reformed at the same time (1951). All the elected members of the Legislative Council were given seats in it, two of them being appointed Ministers without Portfolio.

Two years later (1953), as the demand for self-government became stronger and stronger, a Consultative Committee was set up which included all current and former members of the Legislative Council, and other leading citizens, thirty-four in all. Under the chairmanship of the Governor, this committee made recommendations to the British Secretary of State; as a result of these, in the following year, both Executive and Legislative Councils were made more fully representative of the people of the Gambia. The former now consisted of a Speaker, fourteen elected unofficial members, two nominated unofficial members, four ex-officio members and one nominated official member, usually a distinguished Gambian civil servant, who was also made a member of the Executive Council. The other members of that Council were four officials and six non-officials, of whom two or three were to be appointed ministers. Thus the Executive Council, as well as the Legislative Council, had a majority of Gambians who had been freely elected by their own people.

In 1956 the Chiefs' Conference was instituted, and met annually so as to provide the kings with a platform for the expression of their views on matters affecting the Protectorate. Four years later a government veterinary officer, whose home was in the Protectorate, resigned his appointment to devote himself to building up a political party. He was Mr Dawda Jawara, who had been educated in Ghana and Glasgow. After the General Elections of May 1960 a coalition government was formed between his party (the People's Progressive Party), and the United Party of Mr Pierre N'Jie, with the latter as Chief Minister and Mr Jawara as Minister of Education. In May 1962, however, the P.P.P. won eighteen seats as against the U.P.'s thirteen; and so Mr (later Sir) Dawda Jawara, as Gambia's first Premier, was given a popular mandate to lead the country back to its sovereignty.

On October 4, 1963, the Gambia achieved full internal self- government with control of all matters except foreign affairs, defence and internal security, in which matters the Governor had the final responsibility. The Gambia, the last of the former British West African possessions to obtain independence, became a fully sovereign nation in February 1965. The developments of 1963—5 are referred to in Chapter 7 (pages 111-113).

b. SIERRA LEONE

Having displayed their new uniforms in the Protectorate, many of the troops of the newly formed West African Frontier Force in Sierra Leone were shipped to the Gold Coast to help the British subdue the Asante (page 33). Then in 1905 the Force was used to protect Luawa, when Kai Lundu of Luawa's successor Fabunde was being attacked by a rival, Kafura, whose base was outside Sierra Leone's boundaries. The following year Daru was made the Force's headquarters, which it remained until 1928. In 1911 and 1912 the boundaries of Sierra Leone, as agreed in 1896 with the French and Liberians, were slightly adjusted to bring all the Luawa kingdom into Sierra Leone, in exchange for parts of the Gola Forest, which became Liberian.

Sovereignty Regained: The Gambia, Sierra Leone, Ghana

Education of a Western type spread into the Protectorate in the form of secondary schools and training colleges. Fourah Bay College was given a Royal Charter as the University College of Sierra Leone in 1960, and the range of its courses extended.

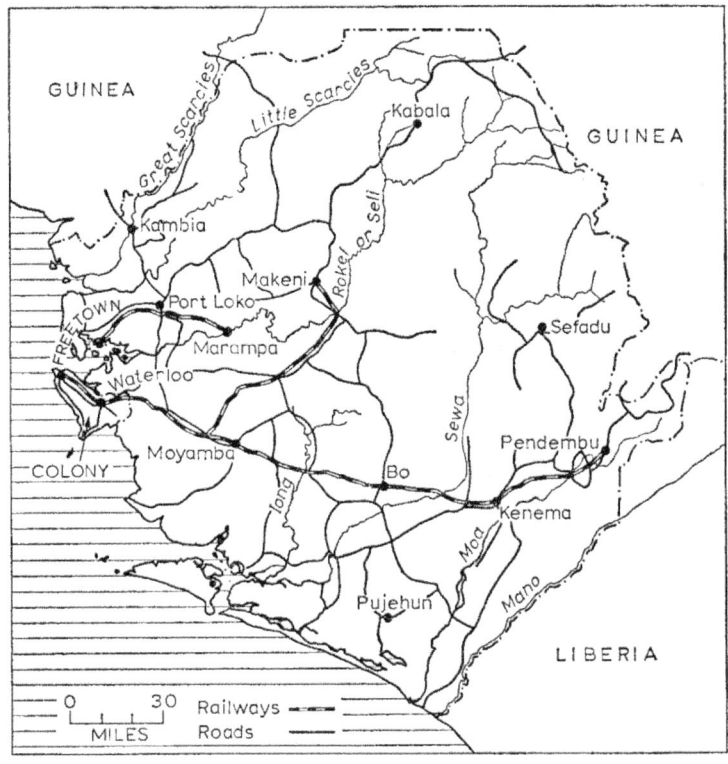

MAP 5 SIERRA LEONE

Meanwhile some progress was being made with communications in the territory. The railway from Freetown reached Pendembu in 1908 and Makeni in 1914. Until 1929 it had a branch line to Hill Station, then the European reservation. The First World War was over before attention was paid to the road system. In 1918 some roads in the colony area outside Freetown were made motorable; ten years later a start was made with road building in the Protectorate. It was not until 1940 that the roads of the two parts of the territory were joined.

In 1924, as a result of a new Constitution, the first since 1863, the first three elected members were admitted to the Legislative Council. The franchise was very restricted. Voters had to be able to read and write and own a certain amount of property. But during the First World War Sierra Leoneans saw service in Togoland and the Cameroons, and during the Second World War others served in

Burma. Like the Gambians, they returned with quickened political interest. The Legislative Council was formed in accordance with the 1924 constitution and consisted of the Governor as president, eleven officials, three elected unofficial members and seven nominated unofficial members, three of whom were 'paramount chiefs', as the British now called the kings. Thus even if the Governor did not exercise his right to vote the unofficial group could always be outvoted ten to eleven. The Executive Council consisted of five officials, one of whom was the Chief Commissioner of the Protectorate. What was worse, Africans were being deliberately kept out of the senior posts of the Civil Service. A lawyer, Sir Samuel Lewis, who died in 1903, was the last African official of real influence until 1945. Forty-five percent of senior Civil Service appointments were held by Africans in 1892, but only sixteen per cent in 1912. This displacement of African officials by British had its counterpart in the social world. In the nineteenth century Creoles and British had mixed on terms of equality, but with the growth of the European colony, largely owing to improved measures against malaria, a social barrier descended.

The Protectorate was divided up into provinces, and the provinces into districts, over which, as in the Gambia, British commissioners presided. In the colony there was a City Council in Freetown, a Rural Area Council for the area just outside and a Sherbro Urban District Council in Bonthe. In 1946 a Protectorate Assembly was created.

In 1947 the Governor, Sir Hubert Stevenson, drew up a new constitution in which he proposed that there should be one government for the Colony and the Protectorate. Africans were to be in the majority in both the Legislative and the Executive Councils. Of the twenty-one elected members of the Legislative Council, fourteen were to represent the Protectorate, with its two million inhabitants, and seven the Colony, with its 60,000 inhabitants. The constitution was bitterly opposed by the Creoles who had long hoped to succeed the British as the governing force. Among the fiercest opponents of the constitution were the veteran Sierra Leonean politician, Dr Bankole-Bright, and I. T. A. Wallace-Johnson, the founder of the African League of Youth, which had worked hard for self-government for the African colonies.

Under the constitution, the Legislative Council was to consist of the Governor as President, a Sierra Leonean as Vice-President (a judge, Sir Ernest Beoku-Betts, was appointed), seven officials, two nominated members and twenty-one elected members. In 1951, despite Creole opposition, the constitution was put fully into force. In the first nationwide elections, in 1951, the Sierra Leone People's Party, formed in the previous year by a merger of Dr M. A. S. Margai's Sierra Leone Organization Society and Mr Lamina Sankoh's People's Party, swept the polls, which were direct in the Colony, and indirect through the district councils in the Protectorate. The S.L.P.P. formed the government, and, in 1954, Dr Milton (later Sir Milton) Margai became Chief Minister. Dr Margai himself

Sovereignty Regained: The Gambia, Sierra Leone, Ghana

was born at Bonthe in the Protectorate. The House of Representatives (as the Legislative Council became in 1956) was again controlled by the S.L.P.P. as a result of the General Elections in 1957. By 1960 no Briton sat on either the Executive or the Legislative Council. At the Conference held in London in April 1960 a United National Party Front was formed by all the political parties to see the country through to independence. On April 27, 1961, the Duke of Kent, representing the British Crown, restored sovereignty to the people of Sierra Leone, represented by their Prime Minister, Sir Milton Margai.

c. THE GOLD COAST BECOMES GHANA

After the defeat of the Asante, the Gold Coast was divided for purposes of administration into three areas: the Northern Territories, which formed a protectorate; Asante which became 'a colony by conquest'; and the rest of the territory which was described as 'a colony by settlement'. The frontiers of the Northern Territory were settled by agreements with the French who completed a long and tedious war with Samori in 1899. The eastern frontier with German Togoland was not fixed until shortly before the war in 1914. On the west the frontier between the Gold Coast and the Ivory Coast was drawn through the Gyaman country. In all cases the frontiers were settled without consulting the African inhabitants and without consideration for tribal divisions. After the 1914—18 war the mandate for part of German Togoland was allotted to Britain, and this area was administered with the Gold Goast and is now incorporated in Ghana.

Economic development

The economic development of the Gold Coast was more rapid than that of the other British West African possessions. Important for this development was the railway which, starting from Sekondi, reached Tarkwa in 1901, Kumasi in 1904 and Accra in 1923. Further extensions have been made since, for example to the new port of Tema.

Gold which gave this part of the Guinea coast its name has been mined there since very early times, but production was declining until new machinery made deeper mining possible and world demand forced up the price. Manganese and bauxite deposits have been worked in the last fifty years, and the latter provides not only exports but also the raw material for the great new aluminium smelter at Tema. Diamonds have been found in commercially profitable quantities, and the forests have provided valuable timber. Important though these products have been, cocoa has been the life blood of the Gold Coast and Ghanaian economy, and it is on this crop that the country's fortunes and ambitions in the future largely rest. It is the world's biggest producer and most of Ghana's farmers rely on it as a cash crop. Exports of cocoa in 1910 were 10,000 tons and in 1957 250,000 tons. It accounts for two-thirds in value of the country's exports. It has financed and will continue to finance many of the developments in education.

Educational progress

In the period before the achievement of independence, education expanded steadily. Cape Coast had an early monopoly of secondary schools but Accra and Kumasi and other towns saw the founding of other secondary schools, for the most part by religious bodies. During the Governorship of Sir Gordon Guggisberg, Achimota College was founded (1925). Under the leadership of the Rev. A. G. Fraser and Dr J. E. K. Aggrey it proved a guiding light in the provision of an education which matched the best European standards and at the same time directed the attention of their students to their African heritage. After the Second World War, the Gold Coast followed Sierra Leone in setting up a university institution: the University College of Ghana was founded in 1948 at Achimota, and in 1952 the Kumasi College of Science and Technology was founded.

Constitutional progress

As in the Gambia and Sierra Leone it was on constitutional progress that most attention was focussed in the Gold Coast in this century. The Aborigines' Rights Protection Society continued the work it had begun in its opposition to the Lands Bill. But the Society spoke for the most part for the Fante chiefs and European-educated Africans and was slow to realize that there was a growing demand for an end to the colonial relationship. In 1907, when a constitution for the Society was drawn up, its objects were stated as being not only the protection of the rights and interests of the Aborigines of the Gold Coast but also the promotion of unity of purpose and action. Stress was laid on constitutional methods and loyalty to the British Crown.

The National Congress of British West Africa

J. E. Casely Hayford, who was, like John Mensah Sarbah, a barrister, continued opposition to the Lands and Forests Bills through the Aborigines' Rights Protection Society; indeed, the action of the Society probably was the cause of the very limited use the Gold Coast government made of its powers for the acquisition of land. The Society, which was based in Cape Coast, had a rival when the movement for West African unity grew. It was through Casely Hayford's initiative and energy that the first West African Conference was held in Accra in 1920 with representatives from Sierra Leone, Gambia and Nigeria as well as a large delegation from the Gold Coast. As a result of the Conference, the National Congress of British West Africa was formed, one of whose aims was the creation of a 'Dominion of West Africa'. It also demanded the creation of legislative councils half of whose members would be elected; control of taxation by those members; control of kings by their own people; appointments to the Civil Service on merit and not race; and the creation of a university for West Africa.

There was opposition to the Congress among Africans especially the Aborigines' Rights Protection Society as well as government officials, and it gradually became more and more unprogressive so that it did not long survive the death of Casely Hayford in 1930.

The constitutional position to 1925

The real power in the Gold Coast under British rule was in the hands of the Governor who from 1850 was assisted by an Executive Council and a Legislative Council, the membership of which bodies was for some years almost identical. In 1897 the Legislative Council consisted of the four members of the Executive Council with the addition of the Chief Justice and three unofficial members appointed by the Governor. However, there was a steady demand for more African representation in the Legislative Council and for representative government; and some training in the responsibilities of government was being provided in the municipal councils set up at the end of the nineteenth century.

In 1916 Sir H. Clifford enlarged the Legislative Council to eleven official and ten unofficial members. Among the latter were paramount chiefs, Casely Hayford, E. J. P. Brown and T. Hutton Mills. This did not satisfy educated African opinion, and the A.R.P.S. and later the National Congress demanded elected members.

The next step forward was the Guggisberg Constitution of 1925 in the drawing up of which the Governor had consulted many Africans. Under this constitution there were to be fifteen official and fourteen unofficial members in the Legislative Council. The unofficial members were made up of six members representing the West, East and Central Provinces in each of which a Provincial Council of Chiefs was established; one representative each from Accra, Cape Coast and Sekondi elected by citizens occupying a house of a rateable value of £6 per annum; three members nominated by the Governor and five Europeans representing various interests. This was a start in the election of representatives but it did not satisfy the A.R.P.S. which urged a boycott. Casely Hayford, who would not stand for election and who led a delegation to London appealing against the Constitution, would not support the boycott which he regarded as unlikely to achieve any success. It should be noted that Asante was not represented in the Legislative Council.

The Provincial Councils and the position of the chiefs

One of the effects of the increased representation on the Legislative Councils was the rise of the influence of the barrister element as opposed to that of the traditional chiefs whose cooperation the British Governors had sought, especially up to the time the threat from Asante was removed. This hope of co-operation was furthered by the payment of stipends to chiefs. The A.R.P.S., which contained many chiefs, became alarmed for their rights both because the Asante threat was removed and also because, with the improvement of health conditions, service on the Gold Coast became more attractive for British District Commissioners whose powers encroached on those of the Chiefs. Nana Ofori Atta, the paramount chief of Akim Abuakwa, realized the threat to traditional loyalties from the government and from educated African opinion. On the other hand the government relied on chiefs in the administration of traditional law in provincial courts from which there was appeal to District Commissioners' courts.

The setting up of the Provincial Councils of Chiefs under the 1925 constitution helped the restoration of the power of the Chiefs. The Provincial Councils consisted of all the paramount chiefs (as the British called the Kings) of the province. They elected their own President who usually represented the Provincial Council in the Legislative Council. Their power was further safeguarded by the Native Administration Bill of 1927 which was the work of Nana (Sir) Ofori Atta who had been a member of the Legislative Council since 1916 and who became a member of the Executive Council in 1943. African opinion including the A.R.P.S. was to a large extent hostile to the Provincial Councils as diverting the Chiefs from their role as spokesmen of their people and leading them more and more to collaboration with the colonial government.

Asante

In 1924 opinion in Asante was to some extent appeased by the return of Prempeh I, though as a private citizen and not as Asantehene. For some years previously discussion had been going on and a number of those deported or imprisoned after the 1900 rising had been allowed to return to Asante, while others had been released but remained in exile. The question was complicated by the continued demand by the British for the return of the Golden Stool. When, however, the Stool was discovered in 1920 and found to have been robbed and desecrated the Asante were allowed to keep it. Respect for African institutions and particularly a better understanding of Asante religion and customs grew as a result of the researches of R. S. Rattray and the governorship of Sir Gordon Guggisberg. The Constitution of 1925 did not apply to Asante and the North, so that the government was dependent on the co-operation of the chiefs; in the North a system of indirect rule on the Lugard model was introduced. The improvement in relations in Asante was furthered when Prempeh I was enstooled as Kumasihene in 1926. On his death in 1935, his successor, Prempeh II, was enstooled as Asantehene.

Sovereignty Regained: The Gambia, Sierra Leone, Ghana

Sir Alan Burns and the 1946 Constitution

Sir Alan Burns became Governor in 1942. He soon appointed two Africans to the Executive Council. Then his government passed laws reforming local tribunals and bringing the chiefs into closer relationship with the central government. A new constitution came into effect in March 1946. The legislature consisted of six official members, six nominated unofficial members and eighteen elected members. Thus for the first time there was a majority of elected members. Of the eighteen elected members nine were elected by the joint meeting of the Provincial Councils, four by municipalities, five from Asante. Of the six nominated unofficial members, three were Africans. Africans controlled the finance committee. The Governor presided but had no vote.

This was a considerable advance but it was not enough. The Governor had considerable reserved powers; for instance he could disallow a bill and he could carry a bill if he held it to be in the interests of good government. In fact the Governor's reserved powers were not used in the eleven years before independence. The great weakness was that all policy was originated by the Governor and his permanent officials - all British - and the Executive Council. All the Legislative Council could do was criticize it.

Deteriorating conditions 1947—9

The period immediately following the introduction of the Burns constitution was one of great difficulty — there were high prices and shortages of goods caused to some extent by the operations of a ring of European and Syrian merchants; there was anxiety among cocoa farmers owing to swollen shoot and the measures necessary to get rid of it; there was a housing shortage; and there was dissatisfaction among returned ex-servicemen about pensions and re-settlement. About these the African majority in the Legislative Council could do nothing unless the government introduced measures. The Opposition party founded in 1947 was the United Gold Coast Convention headed by Dr J. B. Danquah who was the paternal brother of Sir Ofori Atta, and who had been a founder member of the West African Students' Union formed in 1925. The United Gold Coast Convention aimed at constitutional advance by constitutional means. Late in 1947 Dr Kwame Nkrumah was appointed the Convention's Secretary.

The opposition had plenty of material on which to work. To counter the high prices and shortages a boycott was begun in January 1948. This was followed in February by an ex-servicemen's march towards Christiansborg Castle. When the procession refused to turn back six shots were fired on the orders of Superintendent of Police Imray, as a result of which two people were killed and five wounded. Then rioting broke out in Accra during which the central prison was forced open, and there was looting and more shooting. Riots also occurred in Kumasi and elsewhere. In all there were twenty-nine killed and 266 injured. Dr

Danquah and the U.G.C.C. declared that the civil administration had broken down, but the latter retaliated by arresting Dr Danquah and five of his chief associates.

The Watson Commission

The Watson Commission was appointed to inquire into the disturbances. Imray was exonerated, as was the government, from any responsibility for the rioting. Among the causes of the disturbances, the Commission's report stated, were discontent among ex-servicemen; frustration among educated Africans to whom the Burns constitution gave no prospect of power or position; the monopoly of trade by Europeans and Syrians; shortages caused by uneven distribution; the cocoa disease and the remedies taken to cure it; the housing shortage; the government's seeming indifference about high prices; too tolerant an attitude to agitators; slow educational development; lack of progress with the Africanization of public services; the suspicion that the government was still aiming to get its hands on tribal lands; lack of an effective agricultural policy, and too much reliance by the government on chiefs' rule. Of these for the ordinary man the cocoa problem, high prices and shortages were the most important. The Watson Commission also held that further constitutional changes were urgently required.

The Coussey Committee

As a result of the last recommendation a Committee of thirty-five Africans presided over by Mr Justice J. H. Coussey was appointed. Its chief task was to work out a constitution which would give Africans the responsibility for policy and legislation. It proposed a legislature of two houses: an Upper House of thirty-eight members of whom thirty-six would be elected, and a Lower House of seventy-eight members of whom three would be officials and the rest elected. An alternative suggestion was a single-chamber legislature two-thirds elected. The vote would be given to every taxpayer or ratepayer of twenty-five and over. The Executive Council would consist of twelve members—the Governor as Chairman and eleven other members, not more than three of whom would be officials. Of these the leader of the House and five others would be designated as Ministers with departmental responsibilities. The Executive would be responsible to the legislature.

The British government while accepting the general principles, including a single-chamber legislature, did not accept all the proposals. It made the Executive responsible to the Governor, and it decided that, as there was as yet no two-party system, the Governor should nominate the six African ministers who would choose their own leader.

Sovereignty Regained: The Gambia, Sierra Leone, Ghana

Dr Kwame Nkrumah and the Convention People's Party

The British government's insistence on the development of a two-party system brought right to the fore Dr Kwame Nkrumah who had graduated at Lincoln University, Pennsylvania, in economics and sociology and had proceeded to the University of Pennsylvania where he studied theology and education, taking the degrees of M.A. and M.Sc., and later having a doctorate conferred on him by Lincoln University. As has already been mentioned he was appointed Secretary of the U.G.C.C. in 1947. In 1948 he founded the Committee of Youth Organizations and in June 1949, having left the U.G.C.C., he founded the Convention People's Party, taking with him most of the U.G.C.C. members. Dr Nkrumah called for *Self Government Now*. He was not satisfied with the Coussey proposals and in January 1950 the C.P.P. called a general strike and a boycott of British goods. In spite of Dr Nkrumah's insistence on passive resistance there was rioting and two policemen were killed. Dr Nkrumah and others were imprisoned — Dr Nkrumah for twelve months.

The 1951 constitution

While he was in prison the government announced the constitution. There was to be a legislative assembly of seventy-five elected and nine nominated members — of the seventy-five, thirty-eight were to be directly elected and thirty-seven indirectly by state councils and territorial councils. The Executive Council was to consist of the Governor as Chairman, three European officials and eight African members of the Assembly with departmental responsibilities. The election was a triumph for the C.P.P. which won thirty-four of the directly elected seats.

Dr Nkrumah was elected in his absence and was released forthwith with his colleagues. He was named Leader of Government Business. The new government was, however, not a party government for three of the most important ministries, Defence and External Affairs, Finance, and Justice, were in the hands of European officials. This the C.P.P. objected to and they also wished to keep the chiefs out of the central legislature and restrict them to local government. Fortunately the Governor, Sir Charles Arden-Clark, and Dr Nkrumah developed a mutual respect which made the transition relatively smooth. On the 21st March 1952, the leader of the Assembly was elected Prime Minister and the Executive Council became the Cabinet. Most of the representatives of the Provincial Councils voted against the appointment.

A local Civil Service was now set up (1952), separate from the Colonial Civil Service. In 1953 the territory was divided into six regions; and local, urban and district councils were set up, two-thirds of whose members were popularly elected and the others representative of traditional authorities. In the same year a more democratic Accra Municipal Council was formed, to be followed the next year by similar councils at Kumasi, Sekondi, Takoradi and Cape Coast.

The 1954 constitution

The 1954 constitution provided for an Assembly consisting of the Speaker and 104 members, all elected on ordinary party lines with no nominated or special members. The life of the Assembly was to be a maximum of four years. There was to be a Cabinet of at least eight ministers and Dr Nkrumah appointed an all-African Cabinet. The Governor still had certain reserved powers, and external affairs and defence, including police, were under his control. Togoland too was within the Governor's province. It was now but a short step to full self-government and independence. The C.P.P. had seventy-nine members out of 104, the Opposition being made up of the Northern People's Party and the National Liberation Movement which was all-Asante and wanted federation. There was a fear that this demand might hold up independence. The British government appointed Sir Frederick Bourne to try to get agreement between the two sides. The elections held in July 1956 gave the C.P.P. seventy-two seats although it was in a minority in Asante and the North. The British government had stated that it was prepared to accept a motion for independence within the Commonwealth if this was passed by a reasonable majority. This the British government held to have been done after the independence debate on August 3, 1956. After the necessary legislation had been passed in the British Parliament, Independence Day was fixed for March 6, 1957, the anniversary of the Bond. Thus the Gold Coast gave place to Ghana, colonial rule was ended and sovereignty restored to the Ghanaian people.

4
Nigeria: from Unification to Federation

Influences in the making of Nigeria

In the twentieth century, the history of Nigeria is above all the story of the gradual creation of a single nation out of many peoples. Many instruments were used in this nation-building. The extension of British conquest and rule, unwelcome though it was, was the strongest single force in binding the many peoples of this vast country together. Other such influences were communications such as rivers, roads, railways, and air transport, the telephone, the telegraph, television and radio all of which helped Nigeria to develop a national pattern. Just as important were political institutions, legislative, executive and judicial; cultural and social institutions such as schools, colleges, universities and hospitals; the *lingua franca*, English taught in the schools and used in public life and commerce; the press, and finally patterns of trade.

The Royal Niger Company and the extension of British rule

In 1885 the Berlin Conference 'recognized' Britain's claims to the Niger, thanks to the last-minute treaty-making of British Consul Hewitt (page 51). In the following year Goldie (page 51) obtained a Charter for his Company (now called the Royal Niger Company) which gave it administrative and peace-keeping as well as trading functions. Like the British Government in the south in 1884, this British Company gradually extended this jurisdiction over most of the north during the last decade of the nineteenth century by a series of treaties. The Company took its policing and administering work as seriously as its trading. It raised a constabulary, and from its headquarters at Asaba was soon in effective control of a very large area of what is today Northern Nigeria. Goldie secured the frontiers of this area by making agreements with other European powers claiming neighbouring areas. In 1890 he made such an agreement with the French, under which he 'recognized' their conquest of Dahomey. In 1893 he made a similar agreement with the Germans, giving up his Company's claims to Chad in return for the abandonment by the Germans of their claims on the lower Niger. In that year, too, all the Yoruba states except the Egba were brought together under a single British protectorate with its headquarters at Ibadan (page 40) and attached to the Colony of Lagos (page 43). We saw on pp. 45-6 how the British Government added Benin to its spreading empire in 1897.

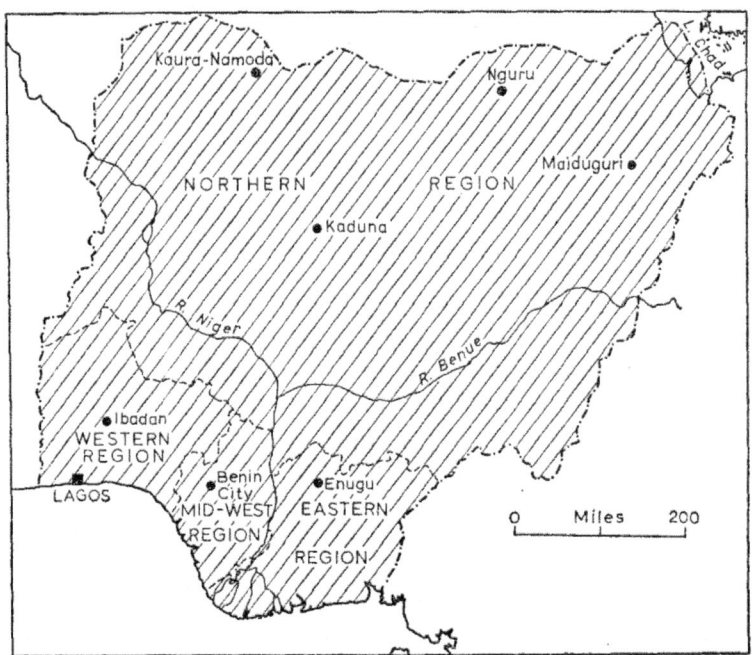

MAP 6 THE FEDERATION OF NIGERIA IN 1965

The British conquest of Benin made it unlikely that the British Government would for long continue to allow a Company to administer and police, as well as trade in, the Niger basin. For the British Government was now set on a course of extending its rule in western Nigeria which would sooner or later bring it into conflict with the expanded jurisdiction of the Royal Niger Company in eastern and northern Nigeria. In 1899, therefore, the Company's Charter was revoked by the British Government, which compensated it financially for the loss of its rights. The Company's territories on the Niger were merged with the Niger Coast Protectorate to form the Protectorate of Southern Nigeria (1900). At the same time a new Protectorate of Northern Nigeria was formed by the British, with headquarters at Lokoja and boundaries agreed by the Anglo-French Convention of 1898. The Protectorate attached to Lagos remained separate, and still included all the Yoruba states, except the Egba (see page 40) and the Emirate of Ilorin, which was part of the Protectorate of Northern Nigeria.

There were many pockets of stubborn resistance to British rule in the east as well as the west and north. One of the most important of these was around the Aro Chuku Oracle (page 49). In 1902 the British sent an expedition to Aro and destroyed the sacred Oracle, which had had such significance for all Ibo people. These people fought back now from many towns and villages: Ogoja, Owerri and in Ibibio country. But although the climate and terrain hampered the work of the numerous British expeditions in these areas during the first two decades of this century, it was only a matter of time before the echoing voice of the cannon asserted its authority. In the west Nupe and in the north Kontagora similarly attracted punitive expeditions by the West African Frontier Force, newly returned from the Asante War.

Sir Frederick (Lord) Lugard, Governor of the Protectorates and Lagos

With the spread of British authority came the influence of a new culture. It is during these decades that a common, and foreign, way of life began to spread over the peoples of Nigeria, as the institutions referred to at the beginning of this chapter were gradually established all over this great area by the British government, missions and firms. In 1906 the Lagos Protectorate was merged with the Southern Protectorate. In 1912 Lord Lugard, who as Captain Frederick Lugard of the Royal Niger Company had in 1894 stopped French encroachment from Dahomey, and who in 1900 had been appointed the first High Commissioner of the Northern Protectorate, was now appointed Governor of both Protectorates and of the colony of Lagos, which had always remained separate from the Protectorates. In 1914 Lugard was given the personal title of Governor-General, and the administration of Nigeria was unified under the title 'The Colony and Protectorate of Nigeria'.

Indirect rule

Lugard's technique for extending British rule in Nigeria was military conquest followed by indirect rule. In this way after the British soldier had imposed his authority, the British government maintained the former machinery of local administration. The North was not subdued without difficulty. Bornu, Sokoto and Kano bravely held out against foreign rule. The Sultan of Sokoto's reply to Lugard typifies the spirit of resistance:

'From us to you. I do not consent that any one from you should ever dwell with us. I will never agree with you. I will have nothing ever to do with you. Between us and you there are no dealings except as between Mussulmans and Unbelievers, War, as God Almighty has enjoined on us. There is no power or strength save God on high. This with salutations.'[1] Dated: May 1902.

So Kano was reduced, and the Sultan of Sokoto pursued and killed. And thus the power of the Fulani Empire was broken. Lugard, however, saw that the vast North could not be held without the Emirs' help and he therefore built up the system of indirect rule with which his name is associated. This system meant that

---

[1] Quoted from Crowder, *Story of Nigeria* (London, Faber).

the Chiefs or Emirs should govern their people as dependent, not as independent, rulers. They would receive their instructions through the Resident, and in their turn would issue orders to their people. The courts would administer native law and be presided over by native judges. At the same time the native law must not conflict with the ordinances of government. Taxes would be raised by the native ruler, who would pay a fixed proportion to the government. The salaries of all native officials would be paid by the Native Administrator. The Resident, and above him the Governor would be a vigilant adviser, not an interfering ruler, and would carefully watch over the rights of the peasantry and see that they were justly treated.

Indirect rule was applied with some success in the west and mid-west among the Yoruba and Bini peoples. But it was unsuccessful in the fragmentary city states of the Delta and among the kingless Ibo and Ibibio.

The last to come under British rule were the Egba; nominally they succumbed when the Egba United Government was dissolved in 1914, but the Egba rose in revolt in 1918. They were finally subdued when troops newly returned from the Eastern Africa theatre after the First World War snuffed out the last flicker of resistance to the British rule in Nigeria.

The Nigerian Council

In 1914, as Nigerian troops were setting out to help the British defeat the Germans in the neighbouring Cameroons (a task they finished in 1916), Lugard was setting up a body to do for the whole of Nigeria what the Lagos Legislative Council did for that city between 1862 and 1922 (page 43) — i.e., advise the representative of the British Crown on the discharge of his duties as the administrator of the area. Like the Lagos Legislative Council, this new body, called the Nigerian Council, had an official majority. Of its 36 original members, only 13 were not officials; and of these 13 only six were Nigerians, including two Emirs. The other four Nigerians were the Alafin of Oyo, and one representative each from Lagos, Calabar and the Benin-Warri area. The other seven non-officials were Europeans representing business interests in Nigeria. The Nigerian Council was not a great success. The Nigerian members particularly did not seem to feel it was worth while attending.

By 1917 the shortage of shipping which was general throughout the world during the war badly affected Nigerian trade, although the world demand for vegetable oils increased and Nigeria could have done well out of her palm-oil had the shipping been available. One noteworthy achievement of these years was the extension of the railway across the Niger at Jebba. The railway system, begun in the early years of this century, was to prove a most important factor in unifying Nigeria.

Nigeria: From Unification to Federation

Lugard's successors

Sir Frederick Lugard retired in 1919. He was succeeded in turn by seven Governors who in general continued his system of rule: Sir Hugh Clifford, 1919; Sir Graeme Thomson, 1925; Sir Donald Cameron, 1931; Sir Bernard Bourdillon, 1935; Sir Arthur Richards, 1943; Sir John Macpherson, 1948 and Sir James Robertson, 1955. Thereafter there were two Governors-General, Sir James Robertson, 1957, and Dr Nnamdi Azikiwe, 1960. The last two were Governors-General of the sovereign state of Nigeria, and Dr Azikiwe became also the first President of the Federation of Nigeria.

During the first thirty years of Nigeria's unified administration (1915—45), it was the World Wars and their effects which shaped most powerfully the course of events in Nigeria. During those thirty years the political movement for independence got well under way. With war-time restrictions removed in 1945, that movement gathered steady momentum, and within fifteen years had triumphed.

The years immediately after the First World War saw some events of political importance. In 1918, as we have seen, the final Egba revolt was put down. In 1920 the National Congress of British West Africa, whose headquarters were in Cape Coast, Gold Coast, formed a branch in Lagos to oppose the method of representation in the Nigerian Council. Because it was a branch of an inter-territorial body, it cannot be called nationalist in the sense in which the Nigerian National Democratic Party was (page 43). But it made its voice effectively heard, and not only in Lagos. In 1920 it sent a delegation to London to petition the Secretary of State, Lord Milner, for a Legislative Council with half its membership elected, and a House of Assembly consisting of the Legislative Council and persons elected by tax payers to protect their financial interests. Sir Hugh Clifford advised Lord Milner to ignore the petition, which the Secretary of State did, and the Governor roundly denounced the N.C.B.W.A. in the Nigerian Council.

The Clifford Constitution

Sir Hugh Clifford was, nevertheless, the author of the 1922 Constitution, which for the first time in British West Africa made provision for African members to be elected to a Legislative Council.

In the following year a new Legislative Council was set up by the British. It had forty-six members, twenty-seven of whom were officials. The other nineteen could in theory vote according to their conscience, but in practice very seldom voted against the government. Fifteen of these nineteen were nominated by the Governor, which fact perhaps helps to explain their voting record. The remaining four non-officials were elected, three of them by residents of Lagos who were British subjects or protected persons with twelve months' residence and £100 p.a. gross income, and the other by a similar electorate in Calabar. With the prospect of contesting these elections, three political parties were formed; the most successful of these was Herbert Macaulay's Nigerian National Democratic Party (page 43) which took all three Lagos seats in 1923, 1928 and 1933. Macaulay's party was, however, chiefly concerned with Lagos affairs, especially with the position of the Eleko, or hereditary ruler of Lagos, who was paid a salary by the British but had no power. As he did not carry out British wishes he eventually lost his salary. At the same time Nigeria was given a new Executive Council. This body consisted entirely of officials, and among its members were the Lieutenant-Governors. All its members sat in the Legislative Council, and, like that Council, it was advisory to the Governor. In practice the Executive Council was a more powerful body than the Legislative Council, meeting more often, and more fully taken into the Governor's confidence. At least the Executive Council did not pretend to be representative of the people: it was frankly an assembly of 'experts'. The Legislative Council on the other hand was obviously defective for the purpose which it was supposed to serve. The North was not represented on it at all; laws passed on its advice had no effect in the North except where they dealt with matters of finance. And it was difficult to have much respect for a law making body most of whose members had not been elected by the people, whose advice could be rejected by a Governor who was himself subject to being overruled by a foreign government four thousand miles away.

The growth of political awareness

However, the four elected members of this Legislative Council were the first four elected legislators in the whole of British tropical Africa; and this constitution stirred dormant political interest in Nigeria. We saw on page 43 some of the results in Lagos. There was a similar awakening in other parts of Nigeria; and, after the Cameroons under U.K. Trusteeship had been brought under the Nigerian administration, political consciousness in Nigeria itself stirred, and with it a greater awareness of the human rights of which the people were being deprived. In 1929, for example, the women of the Aba and Owerri divisions revolted because they feared the introduction of taxation of women following a census of women, children and animals by a warrant (or appointed) chief. Fierce riots broke out and these spread to Calabar and Opobo where the police opened fire on December 17, 1929, killing thirty-two and wounding thirty-one people. The revolt was thus put down, but firing on defenceless crowds was a policy that would lead to the eventual failure of the imperial power. The official Commission of Inquiry exonerated the officials concerned, but a new Commission appointed with wider membership including two African barristers condemned the system of indirect rule through warrant chiefs in Eastern Nigeria.

The 1930s saw several important developments in Nigeria. There was an economic depression in Europe and America, with a lot of unemployment, and too little money and too few goods in circulation. This made the British more

Nigeria: From Unification to Federation

than ever determined to keep those colonies which, like Nigeria, offered them both the raw materials and the markets they needed to raise themselves out of the depression. Nigerians also suffered directly from the effect of the depression on employment and trade, and it sharpened the sense of grievance of many against British rule. In 1934 Ernest Okoli, J. C. Vaughn, Samuel Akinsanya and H. O. Davies had formed the Lagos Youth Movement, and it was this Movement which in 1936 changed its name to the Nigerian Youth Movement (page 43).

The late 1930s also brought before the Nigerian public for the first time the name of the present President, Dr Nnamdi Azikiwe. Born in Zungeru in Northern Nigeria in 1904, the son of an Onitsha civil servant, he attended and taught in mission schools, then worked as a government clerk in Lagos, before taking the then almost incredible step of going to the United States for further studies. But, what seemed an act of lunacy to the colonial powers and their institutions in Lagos (King's College would not accept his M.A. (Columbia) and M.Sc. (Pennsylvania) as qualifying him to teach there) appeared to some others a declaration of faith in the principles for which the United States and its Constitution stand. In 1935 the future President joined the staff of the Accra Morning Post as editor. Two years later, having been convicted with Wallace-Johnson of Sierra Leone for sedition, he obtained a quashing of the conviction, and then returned to Nigeria (1937) and joined the Nigerian Youth Movement (1938) which now replaced the Nigerian National Democratic Party as the popular nationalist party and election winner of the day. However, the only elections to be won at the time were still those to the Lagos Town Council (page 43) and to the four elected seats in the Legislative Council.

The 1930s also saw the linking of Nigeria by a direct air mail service with the U.K. (1936), which was a great advance in communications; the substitution of Chief Commissioners for Lieutenant-Governors (1935), and the division of the Southern Province into an Eastern and a Western Province (1939). In 1938 Messrs Orizu, Mbadiwe, Ojike and nine others, inspired by Dr Azikiwe's example, left Nigeria for Lincoln, Pennsylvania, where in due course they were to be joined by a group of Gold Coasters similarly inspired which included Messrs Nkrumah, Ado Adjei and Jones-Quartey

The Second World War slowed both the political movement and economic progress. But it halted neither. Under pressure from the Nigerian Youth Movement, the Governor, Sir Bernard Bourdillon, drafted proposals for constitutional changes which would bring representatives of the North into the Legislative Council (as distinct from the Nigerian Council – see page 74) for the first time. These proposals also provided for the setting up of regional advisory councils in addition to the central legislative council in Lagos. This was a step, though a small one, towards giving Nigerians more say in managing their affairs.

Sir Bernard Bourdillon led Nigerians to believe that after the war he would arrange for full discussion of proposals for constitutional change before attempting to implement them. Sir Bernard probably had every intention of doing this; but his successor, Sir Arthur Richards, decided to consult only his Chief Commissioners and the Sultan of Sokoto.

The Richards Constitution

Thus the 'Richards Constitution', which came into effect on January 1, 1947, was the creation of the British government and was from the start unpopular. It was applied to the whole of Nigeria. Under it the Legislative Council consisted of the Governor, thirteen ex-officio members, three nominated officials, twenty-four nominated unofficial members and four elected members, two each for Lagos and Calabar. Of the twenty-four nominated unofficial members, three represented special interests not otherwise represented, one the Colony, and twenty were nominated on the advice of the regional councils. The Governor presided and had only a casting vote, but he could carry a Bill even if the Council refused to pass it if, in his opinion, it was necessary for public order and good government. This Council had no control over the Executive, and therefore the constitution was unlikely to satisfy any Nigerians.

One of the novel features of the Richards Constitution was the creation of three Regions, North, West and East. The Northern Council had two Chambers: a House of Chiefs and a House of Assembly, the latter having no elected members, the former including all first-class chiefs and not less than ten second-class chiefs elected by their fellows. In the West and East there was only a House of Assembly; in the West this consisted for the most part of chiefs, in the East of chiefs or representatives of native administrations, with five special members in each case. In Lagos and Calabar the electorate was restricted to persons earning not less than £50 per annum which was by this measure twice as democratic as the 1923 suffrage (page 75).

The regional councils had limited powers: they could neither vote money nor refuse. They were given a preliminary view of bills which were going to be introduced in the Nigerian Legislative Council, for which body they nominated the regional representatives Their chief asset was that they gave Africans an opportunity to discuss public affairs, but discussion without the right to act gave no satisfaction. Africans were not likely to be content with assemblies that were no more than sounding boards for the Governor in Lagos, who could ask their opinion on any matters he chose, but was not in any way bound to accept their advice.

Post-war development

Although the Second World War had led to increased demand for Nigeria's tin and fats, economic progress, on the whole, was slowed down. As soon as the war ended, an attempt was made to recover lost ground. In April 1946 a £55 million ten-year Development Plan was launched, and attempts were made regionally as well as nationally to improve economic conditions and the standard of living of the people. In 1949 Regional Production Boards were established, and Marketing Boards to handle agricultural products.

The need for Nigerians trained to direct the country's economic, social and administrative activities was constantly brought before the Government. In 1948 a Commission, of which Dr Azikiwe was a member, was set up to advise on the training of Nigerians for the Civil Service. In the same year University College, Ibadan (now the University of Ibadan) was established and was soon accepted as one of West Africa's leading institutions of higher education. Its Faculty of Agriculture was in 1950 assisted by a gift of £1 million from the Cocoa Marketing Board.

Dr Azikiwe takes the lead

Dissatisfaction with the Richards constitution was from the first intense. At first criticism was levelled at the failure to keep Bourdillon's promise of wide consultation, and Bourdillon himself joined in this criticism. Later Nigerians subjected the constitution itself to intense criticism. Herbert Macaulay took a lead in this criticism until his death at Kano in May 1946 when on a tour of the North with Dr Azikiwe. Dr Azikiwe now took the leadership in the campaign for Nigerian independence. His party, the National Council of Nigeria and the Cameroons, was totally against the Richards constitution, whereas the Nigerian Youth Movement urged that it be given a trial. A proposed delegation to protest against the constitution broke up through internal disagreements, but the N.C.N.C. captured the three elected Lagos seats and then agreed to try out the constitution.

Moves towards self-government

Then at the end of 1947 and the beginning of 1948 there was a chain of events of profound importance for the history of Nigeria. The British Labour Party had come to power two years before, but had been able to do little to carry out its war-time promises to grant independence to all colonies desiring it. In November 1947 a conference of British Governors in West Africa was held in London under the chairmanship of Mr Arthur Creech-Jones, Labour Colonial Secretary. Among those present were the retiring Governor of Nigeria, Sir Arthur Richards, the new Governor, Sir John Macpherson, and Mr Hugh Foot, the new Chief Secretary. There is no doubt that at this conference the Labour minister told the representatives of the King in clear terms that they must implement faithfully the new policy of colonial freedom.

Macpherson had not even taken up his new post when rioting broke out in Accra which led to the death of some ex servicemen (February 1948) and to the appointment of a Commission whose Report (the Watson Report) made it clear that the pressures of self-government in West Africa were irresistible. In April

1948 Macpherson arrived in Nigeria; and it was he who surprisingly appointed the 'rebel' Dr Azikiwe to a Nigerianization Commission; and announced that the Richards constitution would be revised in 1950 instead of 1956, the date Richards had set for the revision.

The growth of parties

As was to be expected in these early days of nation-forming in Nigeria, nationalism often took on a tribal appearance, indeed the Richards constitution seemed to encourage this. The final goal of all the organizations which will now be mentioned was to free their members from the colonial yoke, not to attack members of other linguistic or tribal groups in Nigeria. At this time healthy tribalism seemed to be of valuable assistance as a forerunner to healthy nationalism, although it later proved to be its enemy.

In 1944 the Pan Ibo Federal Union was formed; and it at once became a strong supporter of the N.C.N.C. Dr Azikiwe became President of both. In 1948 the Pan Ibo Federal Union became the Ibo State Union. Similarly the Yoruba formed the Egbe Omo Oduduwa in 1945, one of the first leaders being Chief Obafemi Awolowo, later the leader of the Action Group. Its first national president was Sir Adeyemo Alakija. A similar movement in the North was the Bauchi Improvement Union. The *Daily Service* was the newspaper of the Egbe, whilst the N.C.N.C. had the *West African Pilot* as its mouthpiece. The Edo, Warri and Ibibio formed similar unions. All these unions sought to stimulate the cultural life of their members and to preserve their traditional forms of dress, art, music and speech.

Soon these largely cultural organizations developed separate political wings. Thus the Ibo State Union became linked with the N.C.N.C. The Egbe's political activities were developed by the Action Group which, like the N.C.N.C., sought supporters from every part of the country. These nation-wide appeals show that the tribal groups were not aiming to break the country up into small unities. The Bauchi Improvement Union was destroyed by the opposition of the Emir of Bauchi and its place was taken in December 1949 by the more strictly political Northern Peoples' Congress, founded by Alhaji Abubakar Tafawa Balewa and Aminu Kano. This won the early support of such hereditary and powerful rulers as the Sardauna of Sokoto and the Emirs of Kano and Zaria. Later Aminu Kano felt this association tended to make the N.P.C. too conservative and cautious, and he formed the Northern Elements' Progressive Union, which was more aggressively anti-colonial.

When Macpherson announced that the Nigerian Constitution would be revised in 1950, a wave of political interest stirred many individuals and organizations to activity. To some extent the activity was directed towards protecting the interests of some particular section, but for the most part it was concentrated in a determination to ensure that all the Nigerian people should be consulted as to the form of the new constitution, and that the new constitution would be a real advance towards independence.

Enugu, November 1949

In November 1949 there occurred what at first seemed a set-back for the movement towards independence. Some members of the N.C.N.C. felt that their leaders were too cautious, and formed a more radical organization which they called the Zikist Movement. It seems that the Zikists may have influenced the coal-miners of Enugu to strike. A detachment of police was sent to collect dynamite stored at the mine. The miners, fearing the police had come to break the strike, rioted, and the European officer in charge, Assistant Superintendent of Police Philips, ordered the detachment to open fire. As a result twenty-one were killed. A Commission of Inquiry found that the officer, who by this time had returned to the United Kingdom, had acted in all honesty, but had shown lack of judgement. Dr Azikiwe unsuccessfully demanded his return to Nigeria to stand trial, and the N.C.N.C. and the Nigerian Youth Movement added their protests against the police action. Disturbances also occurred in Aba, Onitsha, Calabar and Port Harcourt, and when in February 1950 an attempt was made on the life of the Chief Secretary, Mr Hugh Foot, the Governor banned the Zikist movement.

The Macpherson Constitution

The Governor, however, proceeded with his revision of the constitution and held consultations throughout Nigeria. Specific constitutional questions drafted by Mr Foot were discussed first in separate towns and villages, then in districts and provinces, and then in regions. (Lagos and the Colony were treated as a separate region for this purpose.) The process of consultation and drafting took from March to November 1949. In January 1950 a General Conference in Ibadan met to consider the draft: of the fifty-three members of this conference all but three were Nigerians. There were unfortunately some conspicuous absentees. Dr Azikiwe stayed away as a protest against what he considered the failure of the draft to reflect accurately the views of the regions. The Benin representatives, including the Oba, absented themselves because the West Regional Conference had refused to forward to the Drafting Committee a Benin request for the creation of a separate Benin Delta state. Nevertheless the General Conference was certainly the most fully representative gathering of the Nigerian people yet assembled. It accepted the draft with a few amendments, and with further amendments it was accepted by the Secretary of State for the Colonies in London and the Legislative Council in Lagos.

The Macpherson Constitution replaced the Richards Constitution in 1951 and came into effect in January 1952. It provided for a central legislature and executive, and three regional legislatures and executives. The central legislature consisted of a single chamber, the House of Representatives. This comprised a

President and 148 members, of whom 136 were elected by the regional assemblies, six were ex-officio members, and six were special members appointed by the Governor to represent communities or interests not otherwise adequately represented. Half the members were from the North. The Executive consisted of a Council with the Governor as President, the six ex-officio members of the House of Representatives, and twelve ministers, of whom each region nominated four.

The regional legislatures consisted in the North and West of two chambers — a House of Chiefs and a House of Assembly — and in the East of a single chamber, a House of Assembly. The regional executive power was vested in the Lieutenant-Governor who was advised by an Executive Council appointed from amongst the members of the regional legislature. The Lieutenant Governor presided over the House of Assembly in the East and the Houses of Chiefs in the North and West, and appointed a President for the Houses of Assembly in the latter regions.

The distribution of subjects empowered the central legislature not only to deal with any subject but to veto regional legislation, even before it went before the Lieutenant-Governor for his assent. Regional legislation could deal only with subjects such as agriculture, education, local government and public health. But the fact that even when it did legislate on subjects on its list, a regional legislature could still have its action vetoed by the central legislature makes it impossible to describe the 1951 constitution as a federal one.

We must note two more of its provisions, one dealing with the Civil Service and one with finance. An Advisory Public Service Commission was set up to deal with all matters affecting public servants and a Revenue Allocation Commission was established which recommended that there should be taxation at both the centre and the region, and that the regions' revenues should be supplemented by the central government on the basis of the source from which the tax was derived, and the regions' needs. Thus half the tax levied by the centre on tobacco was returned to the region from which it was derived, and the greater the regional population of tax-payers the greater the grant from the centre to that region.

Troubles following the application of the Macpherson Constitution

Though the 1951 constitution was well planned, and the result of wide consultations, it did not result in full co-operation by the various parties. The N.P.C., for instance, were conscious of the educational, social and political backwardness of the North, and feared Southern domination. At the centre, as there was no real ministerial responsibility, ministers only acted as spokesmen for their department in the House of Representatives, and in vital matters such as defence and foreign policy the power was still concentrated in the Governor's hands. Whilst the leaders of Nigeria's political parties knew where they stood in

Nigeria: From Unification to Federation

the regional assemblies, none of them could be certain of a majority at the centre. As a result the leaders of the N.P.C. and the Action Group, the Sardauna of Sokoto and Chief Awolowo respectively, decided to remain in the regional governments. Dr Azikiwe did try to enter the central government, but his effort failed partly because of a rift in his party. This rift resulted in a breakdown of N.C.N.C. discipline and the expulsion of the four ministers it had sent to the central government. There were also troubles in the Eastern regional government which led to such dissension in the N.C.N.C. that the N.C.N.C. government broke up and a minority government was formed by the newly-created National Independence party of Professor Eyo Ita, with the support of the Action Group and the United National Party of Mr A. Ikoku. The N.C.N.C., however, united to block the measures of this government, and the Lieutenant-Governor, after using his reserve powers to carry on the administration, dissolved the wrangling assembly. In the fresh election Dr Azikiwe and his supporters won a decisive victory.

This unhappy start in the East was followed by a crisis at the centre. On April 1, 1953, Chief Anthony Enahoro, an Action Group backbencher, introduced a private member's bill in the House of Representatives, which, in effect, demanded self-government for Nigeria in 1956. The Council of Ministers had by a majority already decided that its members should not take part in the debate on this matter: its official and northern members voting against taking part, the eastern members being neutral, and the western members voting to participate. This voting showed the degree to which Nigeria was still thinking regionally even though the constitution concentrated so much of the power in Lagos. When the bill was tabled the four western ministers resigned rather than accept any part in the collective responsibility for silence on this important issue.

The Sardauna of Sokoto followed this by proposing the cautious amendment of 'as soon as possible' instead of '1956'. This brought about combined action by the N.C.N.C. in the East and the Action Group in the West against the British and the North as delayers of independence. The Council of Ministers was in a weak position since the western ministers had resigned and the eastern ministers represented the minority National Independence Party. When the North asked for regional independence from the centre in all things but defence and external affairs, the breakdown of the Macpherson constitution seemed imminent.

In May 1953 Chief S. L. Akintola, one of the leaders of the Action Group, proposed to make a tour of Kano to explain the West's point of view on independence. Though the Resident banned the tour at the last moment, serious riots broke out in the Sabon-Gari (strangers' quarter), outside the walls of Kano, between the Hausas and the substantial Ibo-Yoruba community. The official figures of thirty-six dead and two hundred and forty-one wounded were probably an under-estimate. These riots were sufficient proof of the depth of the cleavage between the North and the South, and led the British Secretary of State for the

Colonies, Mr Oliver Lyttelton, to announce a conference for the redrafting of the Nigerian constitution to allow greater regional autonomy.

Many difficulties, misgivings and reservations on the part of the delegations of the different regions made even the assembling of a conference in London unlikely. But at length representatives were gathered together, first in London in August 1953, and then in Lagos in January 1954. In the event, the amount of agreement was greater than could have been hoped for. In the federal constitution agreed to by the three main parties, the residual powers (i.e. the powers not specifically allocated) were to rest with the regions. It was agreed that the City of Lagos should be federal territory; this avoided trouble which was likely to arise from the claim that it should be included in the Western region. The Southern Cameroons, another likely source of trouble, was separated from the East. The demand for independence in 1956 was side-tracked by leaving regions free to claim independence for themselves in 1956, but allowing no claim for it in that year for the federation.

The 1954 constitution

The new constitution which came into effect on October 1, 1954 set up the Federation of Nigeria consisting of the Northern, Western and Eastern Regions, the Southern Cameroons and the Federal Territory of Lagos. There was a Governor-General of the Federation and there were Governors of the Regions and a Commissioner for the Southern Cameroons. The Council of Ministers was presided over by the Governor-General and consisted of the three official members of the House of Representatives and three members from each region, with one from the Southern Cameroons. These ministers were appointed by the Governor-General from among the elected members of the Houses of Assembly and on the advice of the respective regional executives, and it is to be noted that there was no Federal Prime Minister. The regional Houses of Assembly in the West and East were now directly elected. The legislature of the Federation consisted of the Speaker, appointed by the Governor-General, three ex-officio members, the Chief Secretary, the Attorney-General and the Financial Secretary of the Federation, and one hundred and eighty-four representative members, of whom ninety-two were from the north, forty-two each from the east and West, six from the Southern Cameroons and two from Lagos. To these were added six special members appointed by the Governor-General.

As has already been mentioned it was now the central legislature's powers that were specified in the constitution, other powers remaining with the Regions, with the exception of twenty-two 'concurrent' subjects on which both federal and regional governments could legislate; in the event of a legislative clash the federal law was to prevail.

The western and northern legislatures had an upper and lower House, the eastern only one House. In the north the House of Chiefs consisted of the

Nigeria: From Unification to Federation

Governor as President, all first-class chiefs, thirty-seven other chiefs, the members of the Executive Council of the Northern Region who were members of the Northern House of Assembly, and an adviser on Muslim law. The Northern House of Assembly had four official members, 131 elected members and not more than five special members. The President of this House was appointed by the Governor. In the West the House of Chiefs consisted of fifty head and other chiefs, members of the Executive Council who were members of the Western House of Assembly, and four chiefs as special members. In the House of Assembly there were eighty elected members and not more than three special members. The Speaker was elected by the House. In the East the Speaker was appointed by the Governor and there were eighty-four elected members. The House of Assembly of the Southern Cameroons consisted of the Commissioner as President, three ex-officio members, thirteen elected members, six members representing the Native Authority and not more than two special members.

The Executive Councils in the Regions were presided over by the Governor, who appointed a Premier who in turn chose his ministers from the legislature of the Region. The Executive Council in the Southern Cameroons consisted of the Commissioner, and three ex-officio and four unofficial members appointed by the Governor-General from the members of the Southern Cameroons House of Assembly.

The Constitution provided for Federal Supreme Courts, and for High Courts for the Regions, the Southern Cameroons and Lagos.

The 1954 elections

In October—December 1954 Nigeria went to the polls to elect a new Federal House of Representatives. To everyone's surprise, except perhaps its own, the N.C.N.C. won twenty-two seats to the Action Group's nineteen in the West. It also won a landslide victory in the East. The Northern People's Congress won seventy-nine of ninety-two seats in the North, extinguishing completely Aminu Kano's N.E.P.U. It now meant that an N.P.C.-dominated Federal House of Representatives was faced by an N.C.N.C.-dominated Council of Ministers, and that the Action Group, which formed the Western Regional Government, had no representatives at all in the Federal Council of Ministers. A compromise was clearly necessary: it took the form of a coalition between the N.P.C. and the N.C.N.C., which gave them 140 of the 184 legislative seats, and all unofficial seats, in the Council of Ministers. They faced an Action Group and United National Independence Party opposition.

Trouble in the East

Thus Nigeria entered the last lap of the race for independence. There were still obstacles to be surmounted. These were illustrated by difficulties which arose in the East, where the Governor had used his reserve powers to restore the posts and allowances of certain expatriate civil servants whom the Eastern House thought the Region could do without. This led to a dispute between Dr Azikiwe and the Colonial Secretary. British banking and commercial interests, worried by the movement to independence and by the success of Dr Azikiwe's African Continental Bank, persuaded the new Governor-General of Nigeria, Sir James Robertson (who had succeeded Sir John Macpherson in mid-1955), to postpone a proposed Constitutional Conference. This conference was to have set dates for regional self-government, and the reason given for its postponement was so that an official inquiry could be conducted into the connection between Dr Azikiwe, now Eastern Premier, and the African Continental Bank. When the resultant Foster-Sutton Inquiry alleged that Dr Azikiwe's conduct 'fell short of the expectations of honest and reasonable people', the Eastern Regional Government and people resoundingly rejected this verdict and gave their Premier their full vote of confidence. Dr Azikiwe, however, prudently transferred his interest in the African Continental Bank to the Eastern Regional Government.

Inspired by the example of Ghana, which had achieved independence in March 1957, the people of Nigeria instructed the representatives of the Federation who attended the final series of constitutional conferences in Britain which began in May 1957 to demand independence for the Federation in 1959.

Economic and educational progress

But before we watch the people of Nigeria taking their final triumphant steps towards the prize of independence, we must look briefly at the economic and social progress they were making at the same time. Between 1947 and 1958 the Central Government's revenue had risen from £14 million to £81 million, and their combined imports and exports from £77 million to £300 million. A beginning was made with the railway extension to link Lagos and Port Harcourt with Maiduguri, with the help of a £10 million loan from the International Bank for Reconstruction and Finance. The potentially dangerous interval between universal suffrage and universal primary education was avoided in the West, which, with more money at its disposal than the other regions, had already introduced free primary education, as had the city of Kano. But the rest of the North is still a long way behind the West's and the East's figure of eighty-five per cent of children of school age actually in school. Universities were planned and opened, beginning with the federal University College at Ibadan which was inaugurated in 1948 and later developed into the University there. In 1958 there were five thousand Nigerian students attending universities and institutions of higher education in the United Kingdom and elsewhere. Today there are five universities: the federal Universities of Ibadan and Lagos, Zaria in the North, Nsukka in the East and Ife in the West. There are medical schools at Ibadan (opened 1957) and Lagos (opened 1961). A valuable report on Higher Education produced in 1960 by a Commission, of which Sir Eric Ashby was Chairman, recommended that places for 7,500 university students should be provided by 1970, and the government raised the target to 10,000. Improved educational facilities are increasing the quantity and quality of public servants in federal, regional and local government.

The 1957—8 Constitutional Conferences

At the 1957 Constitutional Conference in London the question of regional self-government was taken first, at the request of the British. The Conference agreed to the Western and Eastern Regions becoming self-governing immediately, and the North in 1959. A request from the East to have a House of Chiefs was also agreed to, as was the Southern Cameroons' request to become a region — in this case the Governor-General was to make the final decision. The House of Representatives was enlarged to 320, and a Federal Senate was created with twelve members from each region including the Cameroons, and four from Lagos, plus four special members. Universal suffrage was introduced everywhere except in the North, where, as in Switzerland, women were not given the vote. Perhaps most popular of all was the decision to create the office of Federal Prime Minister, on whose advice (instead of that of the regional governments) the other members of the Council of Ministers would be appointed by the head of state, now to be called Governor-General. A decision on a firm date for federal independence would of course have been even more popular; but to this Britain would not commit herself without, she insisted, receiving a request for it from the newly reconstituted House of Representatives.

So in August 1957 the East and West became self-governing, the East holding no celebrations for what Dr Azikiwe considered an incomplete achievement, and the West holding only modest ones — further proof of the fact that the people of Nigeria were now really thinking nationally instead of regionally. In September Alhaji Sir Abubakar Tafawa Balewa became first Federal Prime Minister, the Sardauna of Sokoto, Dr Azikiwe and Chief Awolowo remaining still in the regional governments as Premiers.

In November Sir Henry Willink led a four-man Commission inquiring into the position of minority groups such as the Edo-speaking people of Benin and Warri; the Middle Belt group of provinces (Niger, Ilorin, Kabab, Plateau and parts of Adamawa); and the Calabar-Ogoja-Rivers or C.O.R. group of provinces in the East. This Commission was firm in its recommendation that no new regions should be created for the present. It argued that to do so would create more problems than it would solve; that, for example, the Itsekiri and Ijaw would gain nothing from being grouped with a Bini instead of a Yoruba majority. It suggested that the interests of all minority groups could best be protected by constitutional safeguards and a strengthened federal police.

In September to October 1958 the final Constitutional Conference was held in London. It accepted the Willink report by a majority, the Action Group opposing a ban on the creation of new regions. As Willink suggested it was agreed that fundamental human rights should be safeguarded in the Constitution as a protection for all individuals and minorities, by requiring two-thirds majorities in all legislatures, regional as well as federal, before clauses affecting such rights could be amended. Also in line with Willink's recommendations it was agreed that a Police Council should be set up to decide on the broad policy of police administration, whilst the day-to-day operation of the Force was to be entrusted to an Inspector-General, who would gradually absorb all local forces into the federal force. The 1957 Fiscal Commission's Report was also made the basis for revenue allocation for the next three to five years. It was also agreed that the people of the Cameroons should decide their own future, both as to their relationship with Britain and as to that with Nigeria.

In December 1959 the final federal elections before independence were held; and with no single party winning an overall majority, the N.C.N.C. again joined the N.P.C. to form the government, whilst the Action Group remained in federal opposition. After the Senate had been set up as agreed, a formal motion asking for independence on October 1, 1960, was passed.

The Independence Constitution

A small, final constitutional conference, representative not of parties like the earlier ones, but of governments, was held in May 1960 to draft the Independence Constitution, incorporating the decisions of the various earlier conferences. It provided amongst other things that the powers of the Governors and Governors-General should only be exercised on the advice of their Ministers; that except for election petitions the right of appeal to the Privy Council should be retained; and that the name 'Parliament' should be adopted for the federal legislature.

On October 1, 1960 the Federation of Nigeria duly became independent, with Aihaji Sir Abubakar Tafawa Balewa as Prime Minister and Sir James Robertson as first Governor-General. It was recognized at independence as a member state of the Commonwealth and on October 7, 1960 became a member of the United Nations. On October 16, 1961 Sir James Robertson was succeeded as Governor-General by Dr Nnamdi Azikiwe, the President of the Senate, who became the first President of the Republic of Nigeria when it was inaugurated on October I, 1963.

5
Nationalism in French-speaking West Africa and the Movement towards African Unity

a. THE NATIONALIST MOVEMENT IN FRENCH-SPEAKING WEST AFRICA

At first sight it may seem that the people of the French-speaking countries of West Africa differ in important ways from those of English-speaking West Africa. On closer inspection, however, it will be seen that the differences are superficial and imposed, whereas the similarities run deep. The languages which separate these two people, French and English, are after all their second languages: the languages which link them, such as Hausa, Fulani, Mandingo, Ewe and Susu, are their mother tongues. Underneath the somewhat different political, administrative, educational and legal systems are common institutions such as the chief and the secret society, and a common cultural heritage of song, dance, art and folklore. And whatever may be the case in the future, for the present those traditional institutions and that traditional culture touch the lives of far more people in West Africa than do any systems borrowed from France or Britain.

Moreover, although there are five English-speaking West African states (Nigeria, Ghana, Liberia, Sierra Leone and the Gambia), eight[1] French-speaking (Upper Volta, Togo, Niger, Mali (Soudan), Dahomey, Guinea, the Ivory Coast and Senegal), and one, Cameroun, with both French and English as official languages, there were not fourteen separate movements towards independence in West Africa, nor thirty in Africa. The movement towards independence in Africa is a single movement, as Mr Harold Macmillan, then British Prime Minister, so clearly acknowledged when he used the vivid phrase 'the wind of change' to describe it. Moreover it is also a movement towards unity in Africa. The result is that the leaders of this twin movement in the various countries are now steadily changing those imported political, administrative, educational and legal systems in such a way that they resemble progressively less the British or French systems on which they were originally modelled, and progressively more each other.

---

[1] Mauritania is not here being considered as part of French-speaking West Africa.

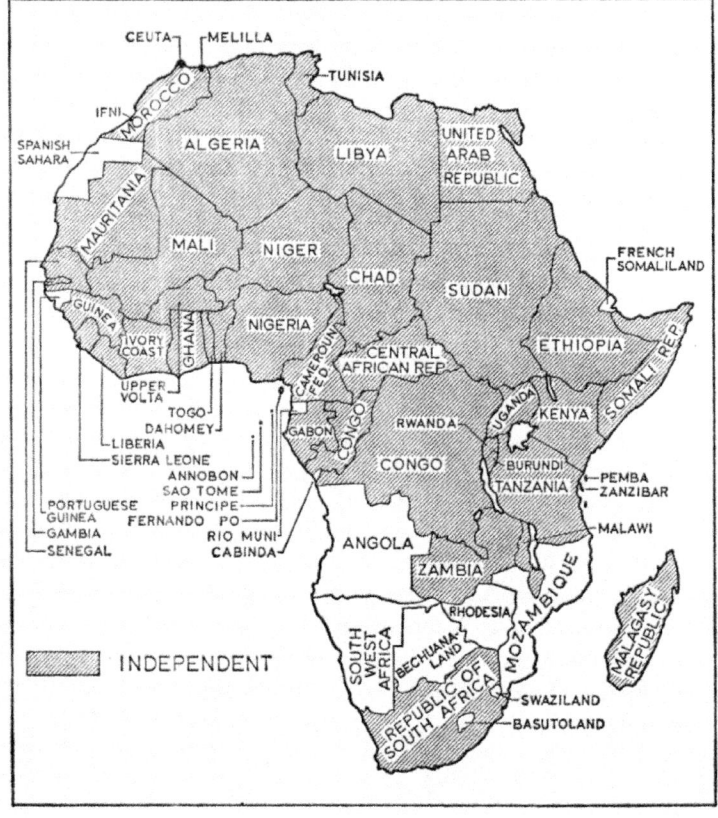

MAP 7 AFRICA TODAY

In other words, whilst the basis of our society and culture remains similar to that of our French-speaking neighbours, even the outward structures built by foreign powers upon that basis, once recognizably either French or British, are all becoming recognizably African. The French Soudan sent representatives to the French National Assembly in Paris, whilst the Gold Coast had its own Legislative Council, presided over by a Governor who represented the Queen. Today both Mali and Ghana are self-governing democracies, with their own particular forms of government, very different from those of the former colonial powers. They are also both enthusiastic members of the Organization for African Unity.

West Africa, which was never more than superficially British or French, is year by year losing more of that foreign veneer, and allowing its essentially African characteristics to be seen by all. The main instrument in bringing about this change is the march towards independence to which reference has just been made. The growth of the movements in English-speaking West Africa has

Nationalism in French West Africa and the Movement towards African Unity

already been described elsewhere in this volume. Here the movement in French-speaking West Africa will be outlined and its effect on the parallel advance towards African unity will be shown.

The area we are considering (see map page 90) occupies most of the north-western bulge of Africa. It covers one-fifth of the total area of the continent, is equal to half the area of Europe, and is eight times that of France. It has a coast-line of 2,500 kilometres, and a relatively low elevation, with few altitudes greater than 1,000 feet, the dominant feature being the broad ridge whose western end consists of the Fouta Jallon Mountains. It is in these mountains that its two largest rivers rise: the Senegal, which flows west, and the Niger, which flows first east, then south.

The vegetation varies, north to south, from desert to savannah to forest. The people vary, again from north to south, from Arab to Negro, and from Muslim to a mixture, in varying proportions, of traditional, Muslim and Christian beliefs. In these respects there is no difference between this area of West Africa and the other areas with which this book deals.

The largest tribes of French-speaking West Africa are the Joloff in the north-west of the area, the Mandingo of the interior, the Fon of the Dahomey coast and the Mossi whose home is along the upper reaches of the Volta. Most of the people live in small villages; but Timbuctoo, Porto Novo and Ouidah are true African towns (not European creations) just as much as Ibadan, Kumasi and Kambia. Most of these people live by farming, fishing or trading, the commodities traded being very similar to those of the rest of West Africa.

The extension of French rule

It was this trade which first attracted the French, like the British, to West Africa. In the sixteenth and seventeenth centuries French traders had set up factories on two islands in the estuary of the River Senegal. Others were soon established along the banks of the river and the shores of the Gulf of Guinea. Traders were followed by officials in the same way and for the same reasons as we have seen obtained in English- speaking West Africa. Until the middle of the nineteenth century these factories had done no more than make isolated and tiny breaches in the sovereignty of the people of the area. Most of these people still lived under the authority of their chiefs, who, completing the simple traditional cycle of sovereignty, were responsible to their people and to no one else. The French traders and officials alike were regarded by the Africans as guests, whose authority was strictly limited to their factories.

This was not, however, the view the French took of their position. The government in Paris defined its policy in West Africa as one of 'amiable pacification'. The French officials in West Africa, impatient at the refusal of the chiefs to take any orders other than trading orders, wanted Paris to agree to impose French rule on the whole vast area between and around the factories, and so create a single French 'colony' which would stretch from Dakar to Dahomey.

Whilst the slave trade continued to yield its high profits to French traders in West Africa, Paris saw no need to incur the very considerable expense which would be involved in meeting the wishes of the empire-building enthusiasts. To trade profitably in slaves it was only necessary to sign a treaty of 'friendship' with the chief, who would then bring the slaves to the factory on the coast or the river. To trade profitably in agricultural produce, however, it was necessary to control the routes between the source of that produce and the factory, since profitable quantities would otherwise be unlikely to reach the factory.

In 1848, yielding reluctantly to international opinion, the French Government declared slavery illegal. It was now faced with the choice of either giving up altogether its factories in West Africa, or of doing what the empire-builders wanted. It chose the latter. In 1854 Governor Faidherbe, openly describing his new policy as one of 'la paix ou la poudre' ('peace or powder'), began systematically and forcibly seizing sovereignty for France in West Africa. Starting from the coast and working along the banks of the Senegal, his soldiers pushed steadily inland. The Berlin Conference of 1885 set off a European scramble for Africa in which France could not afford to be left behind. French officers moved north from the factories on the Guinea Gulf to join those moving east from Senegal, and by the end of the nineteenth century they had completed their task — the acquisition by France of an African empire.

L'Afrique Occidentale Francaise (A.O.F.)

At first this empire took the form of a number of separate 'protectorates', French power in theory protecting that of the chief. These protectorates were linked in 1904 in a federation called L'Afrique Occidentale Francaise, with headquarters in Dakar. Most chiefs quickly showed how much they disliked French protection, and the French decided that direct colonial rule alone would enable them to hold on to, and obtain any profit from, their new empire. The chiefs were gradually confined to ceremonial and religious functions; and an elaborate administrative structure was set up. In Paris there was the National Assembly, to which the French government was responsible. One of the members of the government was the Minister for the Colonies. He exercised authority over a Governor-General for French West Africa, whose headquarters were at first in St Louis, later in Dakar. The Governor-General in turn controlled the Governors who were the chief administrators of the six or seven colonies (Upper Volta was for a time divided administratively between Soudan, the Ivory Coast and Niger). The first Governor-General, appointed in 1895, was also Governor of Senegal; but the posts were separated in 1902.

Each of these Governors had an administrative council. These councils were very much like the Legislative Councils of British West Africa, numerically

Nationalism in French West Africa and the Movement towards African Unity

evenly balanced between official members and unofficial, giving the appearance of African participation in the process of government, but with the effect, and probably the intention, of stifling rather than providing a forum for criticism. The unofficial members were French citizens, elected for this purpose by their fellow citizens. It was not necessary to be a European to qualify for citizenship; but it was necessary for an African to have a certain level of education or a certain amount of property, and also the 'right' attitude towards France. The latter was perhaps the most important qualification; and by 1939 only 2,136 of the fifteen million Africans in French West Africa had become citizens, although many tens of thousands had the necessary educational and property qualifications, and the first Senegalese had become citizens as long ago as 1848.

Most of these administrative councils were purely advisory. However, that of Senegal was given certain limited legislative and executive powers, and so served as the training ground for African politicians. It was more important for the training it gave these pioneers than for its effect on the administration of Senegal. The Governor-General of the federation was very careful to retain tight control over the administration of all the colonies through the Governors. Indeed in matters such as defence and security, customs and excise, the Governor-General acted directly, not through the Governors.

As well as providing African politicians with an outlet for their feelings in these administrative councils, the French provided them with the opportunity to sit in the French Parliament. If the aim was to distract their attention from local issues in West Africa, the effect was to give these politicians a thorough training in practical politics. In the same year in which slavery was abolished and citizenship offered to Senegalese, 1848, these new citizens were offered for the first time representation in the French National Assembly, under the constitution of the Second French Republic.

Another training ground for future African nationalist politicians was provided by the civil service and the other professions of French West Africa — and again this was by accident rather than design. The civil service was divided into an upper and a lower cadre. Officials in the upper cadre were regarded as being in a unified service covering the whole federation, and liable to be sent to serve in any part of it. This brought them into contact with well-educated Africans in other parts. They exchanged views and experiences, and discovered a common but hidden resentment of the foreign domination imposed by the very governments they served.

The same was true of teachers and doctors, and members of the other professions. For although the primary schools of French West Africa served the particular colony where they were situated, the secondary and technical institutions served the whole federation. Most qualified teachers, for example, had been trained in the famous École Normale William Ponty in Dakar, and must often have discussed questions such as colonialism and independence during the course of their training. Most doctors were trained in Dakar University's School of Medicine, and that University also produced lawyers and engineers.

The 'Évolués'

In fact an intellectual elite was being created in French West Africa which the French authorities hoped would be converted by their French-type education into black Frenchmen ('évolués') who would apply for French citizenship, and elect to and be elected to the National Assembly in Paris. The French hoped this élite would forget that for every 'évolué' there were a thousand Africans without any privileges or rights whatsoever — no education, no vote, not even a voice in local government. The aim at this time was 'assimilation', the acceptance by the intellectual élite of French ideals and culture, rather than free association between the people of France and those of West Africa.

The beginnings of parties

It was this very professional class of French-speaking Africans that founded the political parties which, to the surprise of the authorities in Paris and Dakar, began to form in French West Africa between the World Wars. From the start, and because of the highly centralized administrative and educational institutions, these parties were inter-colonial in membership. The Socialists increased their numbers steadily during the 1930s and 1940s under the leadership of Lamine Guèye in Senegal, Yacine Diallo in Guinea and Fily Dabo Sissoko in Soudan, and by 1946 were very influential in the Constituent Assemblies which were discussing the French Constitution in Paris. Although the founders of this party were intellectuals, their main support soon came from the trade unions set up in 1937 in Senegal and Soudan. The party regarded social and political privilege as its chief enemy. In Senegal it began as a Senegalese section of the French Socialist Party (S.F.I.O.) but later under the leadership of M. Leopold Senghor a separate organization, the 'Bloc Democratique Sénégalais', was formed. Similar party developments were the 'Syndicat Agricole Africain' in the Ivory Coast, which provided the nucleus for the 'Parti Démocratique de la Côte d'Ivoire' founded in 1945, the 'Parti Progressiste Soudanais' and the 'Comité d'Entente Guinéenne'. It was not only manual workers who took part in nationalist movements, for example in the Soudan the Graduates' General Congress was founded in 1937. This developed political aims, and was extended to include primary school leavers.

The 'Rassemblement Démocratique Africain' (R.D.A.)

It was, however, the end of the Second World War and the release of energies generated by military service and the Resistance movement that gave the greatest impetus to the expression of African nationalism by peoples under the French rule. Following the rejection of the first draft of the constitution of the French

Nationalism in French West Africa and the Movement towards African Unity

Republic, under Article 41 of which the colonies would have been free to choose their constitutional relationship with France, and the promulgation of the Union of the French Republic which bound the colonies closely to Metropolitan France, both the intellectual and the trade union elements feared that French colonial policy would take away from rather than add to the limited political rights they enjoyed. The emphasis was still on assimilation not free association. At a congress held in Bamako in October 1946 the 'Rassemblement Democratique Africain' (R.D.A.) was formed with the policy 'Equality of political and social rights, local democratic assemblies, and a freely agreed union of the peoples of Africa and the peoples of France'. This policy was certainly effective; in the French elections later that year the R.D.A. secured seats for six deputies, five senators and seven councillors. The most important figure in the organization was Houphouet-Boigny and its stronghold was the Ivory Coast.

Like the N.C.N.C. in Nigeria, the S.L.P.P. in Sierra Leone and the U.G.C.C. in the Gold Coast, the R.D.A. set out at first to be not so much a single party as 'a broad political organization, including within itself all sorts of ideology, open to every national group, to men of all social conditions, and every territory, grouped around a programme of concrete, definite aims' (the R.D.A.'s own definition of its structure). However, although the Socialist leaders played a prominent part in founding the R.D.A., it seemed inevitable that rifts should appear in so broad-based and far-flung an organization. M. Houphouet-Boigny, in spite of his connection with the farmers' organization (the Syndicat Agricole Africain) in the Ivory Coast, said openly that he helped to set up the R.D.A. for reasons of convenience, not ideology. When the R.D.A. not only allied with the French Communist Party but adopted some of the latter's methods of organization, the Socialist leaders broke away from it. African Socialists seem no more willing than British or French Socialists to be too closely associated with Communists.

When the Communists and R.D.A. parted company, R.D.A. found its true mission in the African independence movement. Its period of greatest influence was in 1956—7 when it was estimated to have 300,000 members in Guinea alone. These were the years when the Federal 'Grand Conseil' in Dakar and the highly centralized administration based on the city were becoming weaker. Differences between M. Houphouet-Boigny of the Ivory Coast, M. Modibo Keita of the Soudan and M. Leopold Senghor of Senegal led to the break-up of the R.D.A. into such parties as the Parti Démocratique de La Côte d'Ivoire and the Union Soudanaise.

The 'Indépendants d'Outre Mer' (I.O.M.)

M. Léopold Senghor was the founder of the third great party in French West Africa after the Second World War: the 'Indépendants d'Outre Mer' (I.O.M.). This started in 1948 as a group of deputies in the French National Assembly who did not belong to either S.F.I.O. or R.D.A., but who wanted to work together to promote political advance in France's overseas territories. They felt that this policy was incompatible with affiliation to a French political party, and aimed at representing in Paris as many of the separate African political parties as possible. The Bloc Démocratique Sénégalais was the most important such member of the **I.O.M.**

I.O.M. acquired considerable influence in French political circles, and, whilst remaining independent of political parties in France, used its influence as a bargaining point to secure from the Mouvement Républicain Populaire (M.R.P.) the political advancement of the overseas territories.

Parties supported by the French Government

The government in Paris recognized that political parties were becoming powerful instruments for moulding public opinion in the French territories in West Africa. It therefore itself sponsored the formation of a number of parties, with the help of the very chiefs whose power it had previously sought to reduce. Three such officially supported parties were the Union Démocratique Tchadienne which also found allies amongst members of the French Gaullist party, the 'Union des Chefs et des Populations du Nord Togo' and the 'Union Voltaique'. It will be noted from the names of these parties that they were to be found in the more northerly territories, where feudal-type Muslim chiefs were still powerful.

The growth of nationalism

So the stream of nationalism in French West Africa had many widely separated sources. The main one was the love of liberty which all men know, whatever their race. But this was fed by liberal education and professional training, by a political apprenticeship served in Paris, by trade unionism in West Africa, by doctrinaire socialism, by officially backed chieftaincy and by the shifting demands of political convenience. And giving character and drive to the movement were the personalities which directed it — MM. Houphouet-Boigny, Léopold Senghor, Lamine Guèye, Sékou Touré, Sylvanus Olympio and Modibo Keita.

We must now briefly describe the course of this stream to the point where it brought independence to all the eight territories and carried them into the wider stream of African unity. In 1944 a congress was held in Brazzaville attended by the political leaders of France and by government officials in French West Africa. The purpose of the congress was to discuss how the eight territories were to be governed in the post-war period. At this stage independence was certainly not considered: the future of the people of these territories was seen by this congress as lying in 'assimilation' with the people of France, and in fact the congress described as illegal any attempt on the part of any of these territories to break its association with France.

Nationalism in French West Africa and the Movement towards African Unity

The Pan African Congress

Other influences affected the attitude of the leaders of French-speaking West Africa in their approach to independence. In 1945 there took place in Manchester, England, the sixth Pan African Congress. This Congress and its five predecessors, held at varying intervals and in different cities between 1900 and 1927, gave the delegates the opportunity to express the identity of interests which united all African nationalists whatever their second language and to proclaim the unity of the movement for African independence. The Sixth Congress was attended by young impatient delegates from Africa itself, whilst it had been the West Indies which had contributed a preponderance of delegates to earlier congresses. Among the delegates were a number who were soon to make history; such as Dr Kwame Nkrumah, Dr du Bois, Dr Kurankyi Taylor, Dr J. C. de Graft Johnson and Mr Joe Appiah, all from the then Gold Coast; Chief H. O. Davies, Chief S. L. Akintola and Mr Magnus Williams (representing Dr Nnamdi Azikiwe) from Nigeria; Mr I. T. A. Wallace Johnson from Sierra Leone; Mr Jomo Kenyatta from Kenya; Dr Raphael Armattoe from Togo; and Mr Peter Abrahams and Mr Marko Hlubi from South Africa.

The Manchester Congress met in a different world from its immediate predecessor, which had gathered in 1927 in New York. With the Second World War over and the possibility of years of economic growth, with the coming of the United Nations and its Declaration of Human Rights, the time seemed ripe for nationalist activity. So whilst the 1919 Paris Congress had merely asked for immediate participation by Africans in *local* government, with a gradual extension, 'as education and experience proceed, to the higher offices of state', the Manchester Congress claimed immediately 'the right of every man and woman over the age of twenty-one to elect and be elected to the Legislative Council...' and 'the rights of all colonial peoples to elect their own Governments, without restrictions from foreign powers'. The strike, the boycott, and, as a last resort, force were referred to as legitimate instruments to use to achieve these objectives.

Other spurs to political advance

There were not many delegates from French West Africa at this Congress, but the resolutions passed nevertheless influenced profoundly French West African nationalists. In 1939 a decree had extended to all Senegalese who had completed their military service the right to vote for members of the Senegal Council, which had certain legislative as well as advisory powers. In 1946, as a result of insistent demands by the nationalists, this right was made available to ex-servicemen throughout West Africa. This step is important because it extended the franchise for the first time to Africans who were neither French citizens nor residents of the communes of Senegal.

From now on political advance in French West Africa was steady. In 1945 African delegates had gone to the Fourth Republic's Constituent Assembly: in 1946 African representatives went to the same Republic's National Assembly and General Councils. In 1949—50 there were some disturbances in the Ivory Coast as a result of differences between the R.D.A. and the administration, during the course of which there were boycotts by Africans of European goods. The resolutions passed at Manchester were beginning to have their effect.

Egypt's February 1952 revolution, and the 1955 Bandung Conference of Afro-Asian states, also had their effect on both the nationalists of French West Africa and on the observant officials in Paris.

The achievement of independence by Ghana in March 1957 was another great spur to political advance all over Africa. A further encouragement was the holding of the First Conference of Independent African States in Accra in April 1958. This was attended by representatives of the governments of Ghana. Liberia, Egypt, Libya, Sudan, Morocco and Ethiopia, all sovereign states. At the end of the same year was held in Accra the first All-African Peoples' Conference, others being held in Tunis in 1960 and Cairo in 1961. Further conferences of African governments were held in Addis Ababa in 1960 and Brazzaville in 1961.

The Fifth Republic and the French community

These developments not only encouraged and inspired the nationalists in the countries of French West Africa to redouble their efforts to achieve independence, but also convinced French politicians that such independence was inevitable. General de Gaulle seems to have accepted this position even before he came to power in 1958 and to have determined to convert the French Union of the Fourth Republic into the French Community of the Fifth. So when the Constitution of the Fifth Republic was drawn up, it provided that all members of the new French Community should be represented in its Executive Council, Senate and High Court. Even more important was the removal by General de Gaulle of the ban placed by the 1944 Brazzaville Congress on the breaking of constitutional links between France and the overseas countries associated with her. In 1959 all these countries were given the choice of saying '*oui*' or '*non*' to the question of entering the community. From now on the emphasis was on association, not assimilation, though the emphasis on French culture was not given up.

The Ghana-Guinea Union

At first only Guinea, led by Sékou Touré, said '*non*'. Immediately Guinea was brought into the main stream of independence and the Pan African movement. It also found itself cut off forthwith from all financial help from France. In May 1959 Ghana and Guinea agreed to form a Union (later for a time joined by Mali)

Nationalism in French West Africa and the Movement towards African Unity

which they hoped would be the nucleus of a Union of all independent African states. In July of the same year President Tubman of Liberia met Dr Nkrumah of Ghana and M. Sékou Touré of Guinea at Sanniquellie; and a declaration issued after the meeting, whilst abandoning the word 'Union' and adopting the looser one 'Community', described as the goal of this new African Community 'unity among independent African States'. It also stressed, however, that each state would maintain its national identity and constitutional structure.

The break-up of the French Community

The seven African states which had voted to become members of the French Community could, if they preferred, have remained territories of France (a relationship similar to that of Puerto Rico with the United States) or become departments of France (as Algeria was described before her independence), rather than becoming full self-governing members. Most of them naturally chose full membership; and even this relationship they only continued until they felt they had become sufficiently self-reliant economically and administratively to follow Guinea out of the French Community altogether. This Senegal and Sudan did later in 1959, forming the Federation of Mali (which Senegal, however, left in August 1960). In the following year the remaining West African members of the French Community also left it.

The 'Union Africaine et Malgache' (U.A.M) — the Brazzaville Group

The former French Community states now held meetings with a view to setting up an organization of their own. As the result of these meetings an organization called the 'Union Africaine et Malgache' was formed in September 1961, the final agreement being reached at Tananarive, at a Congress presided over by Léopold Senghor of Senegal and attended by the heads of state of ten countries with the Foreign Minister of the Central African Republic and the President of the National Assembly of the Ivory Coast. The purpose of the Union was to facilitate co-operation in various fields between Congo (Brazzaville), the Ivory Coast, Mauritania, Upper Volta, Dahomey, Chad, Gabon, the Central African Republic, Cameroun and the Malgache Republic (Madagascar). A general secretariat was set up in Cotonou and another secretariat in New York to assist the permanent U.N. delegations of the member states. Co-operation was also organized in economic affairs, defence, posts and telecommunications, airlines and banking. In May 1962 a West African Monetary Union was set up and an agreement made in Paris whereby the C.F.A. (Communauté Financière Africaine) franc would be at par with the French franc; Mali, however, withdrew almost at once in June 1962 and set up her own Bank of issue while remaining in the franc area. The Union which came to be known as the Brazzaville group, was extended in 1963 by the admission of Rwanda and Togo, making a total of fourteen members.

b. THE ORGANIZATION OF AFRICAN UNITY

The Brazzaville, Casablanca and Monrovia groups

The U.A.M. was not the only demonstration that African states were not only regaining sovereignty but were forging a new unity. The Ghana-Guinea-Mali and the Ghana-Guinea-Liberia Community, though both short-lived, were others. The 'Conseil de l'Entente' of Dahomey, the Ivory Coast, Niger and Upper Volta was formed in April 1960 under the leadership of M. Houphouet-Boigny. This group continued to work inside the Brazzaville Group, the U.A.M. It worked in close economic and cultural association with France, and was generally pro-Western in outlook. Looking towards the East rather than the West, and accepting Communist aid and often favouring Communist methods, was another group of states, the Casablanca group, Morocco, Ghana, Guinea, Mali (formerly Soudan), the United Arab Republic, Tunis and Algeria which could be said to have grown out of the Ghana-Guinea-Mali Union. It differed from the Brazzaville group on such issues as the Morocco-Mauritania dispute, the feuds in Congo (Leopoldville) and Algeria's war with France. In May 1961 the Brazzaville group was enlarged by a link-up with Nigeria, Liberia, Somalia, Sierra Leone, Ethiopia and Libya to form the Monrovia group. This loose association took a firmer shape at a meeting in Lagos in January 1962 which was also attended by representatives of the Congo (Leopoldville). Here the Charter of an Organization of Inter-African and Malagasy States was drawn up. In March 1962 the Brazzaville Heads of State met in Bangui in the Central African Republic and agreed to take a full part in the work of this new Organization, but to retain within it their own association. In June 1962 at a meeting of Foreign Ministers of the new Organization held again in Lagos, a draft Charter was approved.

Other moves towards African unity

Other bodies working for African co-operation were the African Trade Union Confederation of U.A.M., the All Africa Trade Union Federation of the Casablanca group; the Commission for Technical Co-operation in Africa South of the Sahara (C.C.T.A.) which was originally set up by European states but was taken over by African states who dropped 'South of the Sahara' from the title and renamed it S.T.R.C.; they barred Britain, France and Belgium from full membership and excluded Portugal and South Africa altogether. An African, Dr Mamadou Touré of Mauritania, was in August 1962 appointed to succeed a Frenchman, M. Cheysson, as Secretary-General of the Commission, which had among its major projects the vital training of middle-level civil servants, and the administration of a continent-wide scholarship scheme.

Nationalism in French West Africa and the Movement towards African Unity

The Organization of African Unity created

It was now only a question of time before the two major groupings of independent African states, the Casablanca group and the Inter-African Organization, each with its associated specialized bodies, came together to proclaim to the rest of the world what so many African leaders have said so often: that the sovereignty of none is secure until the sovereignty of all has been secured, and that African unity is the only real instrument for securing both. There had never been any disagreement amongst African states over ends, merely over means; and in May 1963 the Foreign Ministers of thirty-one independent African states met at Addis Ababa to prepare the ground for a meeting in the same city later in the month of their Heads of State and Government. The only absentees were Togo (whose President had been assassinated in circumstances which led to sharp differences between the other African governments as to the legality of the appointment of his successor) and Morocco (whose King Hassan feared that his attendance at a conference with the Head of State of Mauritania might be taken to imply recognition of the sovereignty of a country Morocco still claimed). Also at Addis Ababa were observers from political parties in many dependent countries of Africa, including Southern Rhodesia, Kenya, Angola, Nyasaland, Swaziland, South-West Africa and Mozambique.

The Addis Ababa Conferences of May 1963 are a most important milestone in the history of Africa. For although important differences of emphasis and priority still remained between the states, an Organization of African Unity was at last created there which was representative of popular opinion throughout the continent. Under the Charter of the new Organization a number of institutions and specialized commissions were set up. These included an Assembly of Heads of State and Government which met in Cairo in July 1964 and again in Accra in September 1965. Meetings of a Council of Ministers were held in Dakar in August 1963, in Cairo in July 1964 and in Lagos (an emergency Session) in June 1965. A Secretariat has been established in Addis Ababa. An important Commission is the Commission of Mediation, Conciliation and Arbitration, and there is a Liberation Committee to promote the achievement of independence by the remaining colonies. The specialized commissions include an Economic and Social Commission; an Educational and Cultural Commission; a Health, Sanitation and Nutrition Commission; a Defence Commission, a Scientific, Technical and Research Commission; a Communications Commission and a Commission of African Jurists. All these Commissions met in 1964—5.

By the time of the Accra meeting of the O.A.U. Heads, the Organization's membership had grown to thirty-six, Togo, Morocco, Kenya, The Gambia and Malawi having all in the meantime qualified and been accepted. Addis Ababa has been approved as the site of the Organization's Permanent Secretariat, M. Diallo Telli of Guinea as its first Secretary-General, and the formula for financial contributions by member states to the U.N.O. as the basis for the distribution of the expenses of the O.A.U. has been agreed. In Accra in October 1965 the only absentees were the four Entente states and Togo, and a firm stand was taken by the thirty-one states present against the threatened seizure of independence by Rhodesia.

The creation of the O.A.U. quickly produced results. In August 1963 a treaty for the establishment of an African Development Bank was signed in Khartoum by twenty-two African governments and was soon acceded to by others. In September 1964 the Bank's charter came into force, and a year later it had a paid-up capital of 32,000,000 dollars. It has now moved from its temporary quarters in Addis Ababa to permanent headquarters in Abidjan. In March 1964 the Foreign Ministers of the fourteen U.A.M. states met in Dakar to dissolve the Union in its old form and replace it by a 'Union Africaine et Malgache de Co-operation Économique' leaving political matters to the O.A.U.

The O.A.U. States one by one applied economic sanctions and communications boycotts against South Africa. The Liberation Committee worked steadily at aiding the liberation movements in dependent African countries, and was re-appointed by the July 1964 Heads of State meeting to continue this work. In September 1964 there was a special session of the Council of Ministers attended by thirty-four of them, to discuss a fresh Congo-Leopoldville crisis. Although the O.A.U.'s intervention here was not effective, owing to the mutual mistrust between the Prime Minister of the Congo (Leopoldville) and some members of the O.A.U., yet the fact that a genuine attempt to mediate in an African political dispute had been made by a continent-wide African organization was very important.

Above all the majority of members of the Organization have agreed that greater political unity is best approached through more effective economic and technical co-operation. Africans are not yet ready to enact, execute and interpret common laws for the whole continent: they are, however, ready to fight together hunger, ignorance, disease, poverty and the last vestiges of foreign rule in the continent.

6
Liberia

Liberia differs from other West African states in that it was never directly subjected to rule by a colonial power. It was the first modern African State of West Africa to become independent. It is a country formed for Negroes and governed by Negroes. In the early days it relied greatly on the United States, and particularly the American Colonization Society, and more recently it has been greatly helped by American aid and interest. Since 1847 it has been an independent Republic; in its history since then there have been times of crisis from which it has emerged safely until it has now reached a position of some influence and a state of stability.

Liberia has an area of 43,000 square miles and a population of about two and a half millions of whom four-fifths are tribal citizens of the interior. It is composed of three provinces, the Western, Central and Eastern Provinces. Behind the coastal area, thirty or forty miles deep, there lies a hinterland which until recently was little known and largely unexplored.

Early history

About 1800, there were in the United States of America perhaps as many as 200,000 coloured men, women and children, slaves who had been freed for various reasons or children of Negro slave women by white fathers. Many of these were in a desperate condition, as were some of the slaves freed in Britain after the Mansfield judgement. A plan for a colony was evolved by the American Colonization Society in 1816; it resembled in some ways the plan for the original Sierra Leone settlement.

Sherbro Island was chosen as the site, and in 1820 the first ship sailed with eighty-eight colonists. Unfortunately Sherbro Island proved unhealthy, and the white leaders and many of the colonists died. As a result the next ship sailed to Sierra Leone where the colonists stayed until a more suitable spot was found. This proved to be land bought from local chieftains on Prudence Island and on the mainland site of Monrovia, named after President Monroe of the U.S.A. The settlement was at first threatened by hostile tribesmen, but a United States war ship, and a few cannon, and a young and vigorous governor, Jehudi Ashmun, gave the colony new strength and hope. Attack came from the Des, Mamba and Vai tribes, but when the climax was reached in the Battle of Crown Hill, November 11 1822, the attack was beaten off, and later attacks were repulsed with British help.

These attacks, sickness and lack of supplies held back the development of the colony and the American Colonization Society sent the Rev. R. Gurley to

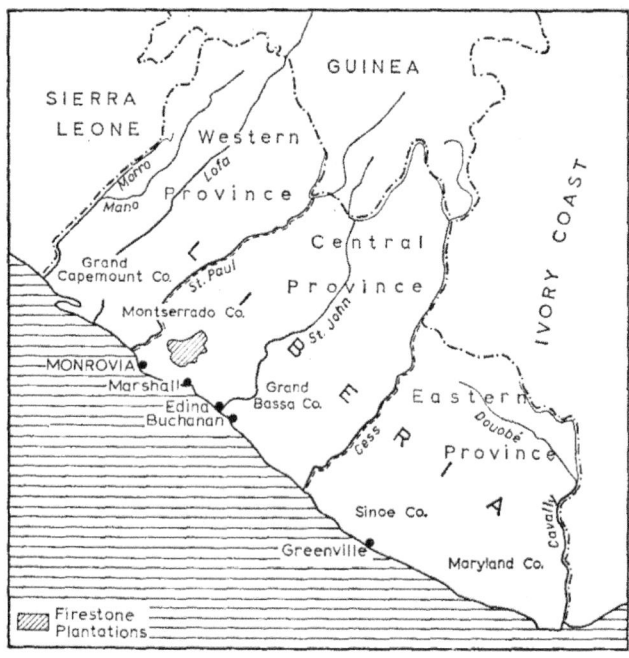

MAP 8 LIBERIA

Investigate conditions, especially the rule of Jehudi Ashmun, who, though he ruled on behalf of the Society, was said to be a tyrant. Gurley prepared a constitution under which the Governor was to be appointed by the American Colonization Society to carry out the orders of the Society, while the actual running of the colony was to be in the hands of a Vice-Governor and ten other officers, all elected. In February 1824 the colony was named Liberia — the Land of the Free.

It was gradually expanded as more freed Negro slaves came. Land was bought from King Freeman and other African chiefs, and in places the area was extended inland into the forest country beyond the coastal fringe. Before 1840 other towns were founded — Marshall, Buchanan, Greenville, Edina. But the colony was still very dependent upon the American Colonization Society as the colonists seemed unable to do very much for themselves.

One of Ashmun's great problems was the struggle with the slave traders. In this, his determined policy was assisted by the British, while the tribal chiefs fought to maintain the slave trade. Ashmun's exertions wore him out so that he died while still a young man. In 1836 a Commonwealth of Liberia was formed comprising all the settlements except Maryland County. The first Governor of the Commonwealth, Thomas Buchanan, had to face strong attacks by Gatumba and Gola tribesmen which were repulsed by the Vice-Governor, Joseph Jenkins

Roberts. He also had trouble with slave trading, and, in his efforts to suppress it, was helped by American warships, which had by this time joined the British anti-slave trade patrols of West African coasts.

Joseph Jenkins Roberts

By 1840 there were 32,000 colonists. In 1842 Buchanan died, and was succeeded by the Vice-Governor and General of the citizen army, Joseph Jenkins Roberts, who became Liberia's first coloured Governor and one of her most famous citizens. He was born in 1809 in Virginia. At this time Liberia was exposed to new dangers from the operations of French and British merchants who sought new trade as a substitute for the trade in slaves. British merchants from Sierra Leone tried to get the British government to take over Liberia which occupied much of the coast between Sierra Leone and British stations on the Gold Coast, but the British government had no wish to extend its colonial commitments. The French also were attempting to buy land on the Liberian coast. J. J. Roberts completed the possession of the coast from Mano River to Maryland County, and also secured the co-operation of the latter which was at this time a rival of the Liberian Commonwealth.

Independence

The time was now approaching when the position of Liberia would have to be considered. Was it to be an American colony or an independent country? Its administration was becoming too difficult for the Colonization Society. The position became acute when Governor Roberts imposed a duty of five per cent on goods brought into the country in order to get funds to run the government. Traders, especially from Sierra Leone, refused to pay. The British government regarded Liberia as the property of the American Colonization Society, not as a self-governing nation, and supported a British captain who refused to pay harbour dues and the import charges. Governor Roberts complained to the British government and sought American help. With some doubts, Liberia moved towards independence, and Liberia's independence was declared on July 26, 1847. The Declaration of Independence is an interesting document. It is clearly influenced by the American Declaration, and it acknowledges the debt to the American Colonization Society. It appeals to all nations for sympathy and understanding, and the acceptance of Liberia as a member of the family of nations.

The constitution was based on that of the United States, with a President, a Senate of well-known people and a House of Representatives — all elected. On August 24, 1847 the flag of the new Republic was first flown at Monrovia, and J. J. Roberts was elected the first President in October 1847. He visited Britain and signed a treaty of trade and friendship, and was received by Queen Victoria. He also visited other European countries, seeking particularly co-operation in dealing with the slave trade. The United States at this time lagged behind in recognition of the new state because it was not prepared to accept a Negro envoy from Liberia. Maryland County did not join Liberia in 1847, but in 1857 asked to be admitted to the Republic and accepted the Liberian constitution. This gave Liberia two hundred miles more coast-line, but the boundaries inland were not defined, and the new state was constantly threatened by British and French encroachments.

Trade and boundary disputes

The chief trade at this time was in palm-oil, but some of the traders added slave trading to their other activities. One of the most notorious of these traders was John Harris who set up his trading base between Sulima and the Mano River. There was a dispute, as a result, over boundaries between Sierra Leone and Liberia, and still further trouble when a gunboat was sent to Monrovia to regain two of Harris's schooners taken by Liberian coastguards. President Benson, who had succeeded Roberts in 1856, went to London in 1862 to try to settle matters. Disputes with Sierra Leone, however, continued until the Mano River was recognized as the boundary, as it still is today. Trading troubles continued. Benson's successor in 1865 named six ports of entry to which foreign ships were to go. Traders, of course, tried to land their goods elsewhere, and often lost their ships in consequence. Further boundary disputes occurred and these were usually settled to the advantage of the French or British. As late as 1910, 2,000 square miles of hinterland was ceded to France. A final settlement of boundaries was not reached till 1911—12.

Financial difficulties

Money was vitally necessary for the development of Liberia. First efforts to raise loans were unsuccessful, partly owing to the unwillingness of bankers to lend, and partly owing to the corruption of President Roye and others in Liberia, which resulted in 1872 in the recall to the Presidency of the veteran J. J. Roberts. He remained in office until his death in 1875. There was, of course, a serious danger that those in Britain and America who loaned money to such an impecunious state might expect excessive privileges in the country. Indeed, the United States, in return for loans, seemed to be exercising more and more influence as the nineteenth century went on, so that by the early years of the twentieth century Liberia appeared to be in considerable danger of losing her independence. She followed the U.S.A. into the first World War in 1918, and had an unpleasant surprise when a German submarine appeared off Monrovia; when the submarine commander's demands were not met, the vessel opened fire causing damage and four deaths before it was chased off by a British armed ship.

Liberia

The inter-war period — the Firestone Company

In the period after the first World War, an all-important development took place when the Firestone Company of America asked the Liberian government for a ninety-nine year lease on one million acres of land, the reason for this being that prospectors had reported that the country was suitable for the large-scale production of rubber, which would relieve America's dependence on supplies from Malaya. The terms were agreed, and in time roads were built, employment was found for Liberians, and the government profited from the rent paid per cultivated acre and a royalty on the sale of rubber produced. American interest was, however, at the same time an advantage and a threat. The Liberian government made attempts to limit this threat by insisting that any Firestone employees accused of offences should be tried in Liberian courts, and by setting a limit (1,500) on the number of white people to be employed.

Liberia's reputation was adversely affected in this post-war period by allegations that contracts had been entered into by the Liberian government with the Spanish authorities to supply labour for the plantations in Fernando Po on conditions that closely resembled slavery. There were plenty of people in America, especially in the Firestone Company, who wished to see Liberia taken over by the United States, and these allegations seemed to justify such a course. A committee was set up by the United States government and the United Nations to look into Liberian affairs, particularly the allegations of forced labour and slavery, and to suggest better ways of ruling the country. An attempt to put in a League of Nations official as a virtual dictator was firmly and successfully resisted by President Edwin Barclay, who himself set about the introduction of effective reforms. This was the last crisis regarding Liberia's independence and sovereignty.

The constitution

Liberia's constitution is adapted from the American constitution with a President, a Senate and a House of Representatives, as already stated. The President is the head of the executive; the Senate is composed of ten members, two from each of the five counties, elected for six years; and the House of Representatives has thirty-one members, five of whom represent the tribal peoples. New laws must be passed by the House of Representatives and the Senate and approved by the President. The President was at first elected for two years, later for four years, and in 1934 a further amendment extended the term to eight years, with the provision that no President shall be elected for two consecutive terms. This restriction has become inoperative, a President is now elected for eight years and may be re-elected for any number of terms of four years. President Tubman is now serving his fifth term of office. The President must be over thirty and have been a Liberian citizen for fifteen years. He is commander-in-chief of the army and navy, and chooses his ministers, subject to the agreement of the Senate. The Vice-President, also elected, takes over if the President is ill or dies in office.

There is a Supreme Court which, like that of the United States, in addition to its judicial duties, examines new laws to see that they are in accordance with the constitution. It can rule that a law is unconstitutional. The largest unit of local government is the county, there being five counties each with a superintendent appointed by the central government — Montserrado, Grand Bassa, Sinoe, Grand Cape Mount and Maryland. The towns are also controlled by officials, commissioners appointed by the President. The various tribes are registered, and the members of the tribe choose a paramount chief, who is allowed a good deal of power under the guidance of provincial officers.

Traditional law and customs

The customs of most of the tribal citizens of Liberia have changed little with the centuries. Their religion is largely concerned with nature, though there are Muslims, and there are also Christian missions with schools, hospitals and clinics in the tribal areas. There are powerful secret societies (Poros) which maintain the customs of the tribes.

The chief crops are coffee, cocoa, ginger, cassava, rice, cotton, corn, citrus fruits, paw-paws, pepper and sweet potatoes. The tribal peoples excel in leather-work and weaving on simple looms. Traditional law is still in force in some areas, with death as the punishment for serious crimes. The very gradual spread of education, the improvement of methods of agriculture, the end of tribal wars and the increase in trade, as well as contact with the central government, has brought the tribes more into the current of life, and has improved their diet and health. President Tubman, who has made the improvement of conditions among all the peoples of Liberia a main plank of his policy, has promised that tribal customs which are not inhuman or cruel will continue and that the rule of paramount chiefs will be respected; indeed he hopes to integrate it with the rule of the government of Liberia.

Economic development

Vast forests still cover much of Liberia, but two million acres are suitable for growing crops such as those mentioned in the preceding paragraph. The Department of Agriculture is anxious to help the small farmers who produce two-thirds of Liberia's rubber, but it is hampered by the fact that thirty-three languages are spoken and only one in a hundred citizens understands English. Liberia is very dependent on foreign help, especially from America, in the development of its resources. It needs not only loans but also technical assistance in planning, surveying, map-making, etc. Foreign loans are also essential for the improvement of administration, communication, education, agriculture and all health services. The American Liberian Mining Company is an example of

American enterprise, in this case in the mining of rich iron ore. Many roads have been built since 1943. Monrovia has been greatly developed as a port, a 'free' port which can be used by merchants trading e.g. with Guinea without payment of customs. The airport of Robertsfield too has been largely built with American capital.

In the Second World War Liberia played a vital role in the defence plans of the United States, and the U.S. still trains and equips the Liberian army. United States interests have thus been greatly stimulated, with the Firestone Company retaining a most important place in the Liberian economy. The U.S. dollar is legal tender side by side with the Liberian dollar.

Recent policy

Liberia has aimed at a policy of steady economic development and of friendly co-operation with its neighbours. It has endeavoured to act as a moderating influence among African states. In 1961—2 Liberia entered a period of diplomatic activity. President Tito's visit in 1961 seemed to indicate that Liberia was not wholly committed to the West. On the other hand, Queen Elizabeth II and Prince Philip visited Liberia later in 1961, and President and Mrs Tubman were the guests of Queen Elizabeth in July 1962. In May 1961 Liberia took the lead in declaring a complete political and commercial boycott of South Africa and in banning South African ships from her harbours and her planes from Robertsfield airport except in emergency.

Liberia has not wholly escaped the wave of plots and attempts at subversion which have swept West Africa in recent years. The most serious plot was that to assassinate President Tubman in February 1963 and one in which the commander of the Liberian National Guard was held to be implicated. Some of the country's economic programmes proved over-ambitious, and in 1963 it had difficulty in meeting its international commitments. The result was increased dependence on U.S. technical assistance. President Tubman's re-election for a fifth term in May 1963 gave an assurance of renewed stability. His policy is to raise the social and economic level of the people of the interior and to give them opportunities on equal terms with the descendants of the original settlers who have so far dominated the political scene; to improve educational standards which have lagged behind those of other West African States; and to integrate the hinterland with the relatively narrow coastal area. President Tubman has great powers under the constitution, and has shown great political skill. He has supplemented American help with special credit agreements and agreements for technical assistance with West Germany and Israel. The name of Liberia has been prominent in the shipping world as Liberia's flag is now flown by the world's fourth largest merchant fleet, composed for the most part of ships owned by foreign companies or individuals and registered in Liberia for taxation reasons.

The country's future will in great measure depend on the development of its natural resources, and the education and integration of the tribal peoples.

7
Independent West Africa: The Commonwealth Countries

a. THE GAMBIA

The disputed election

When the Gambia, Britain's oldest, smallest and last possession in West Africa was moving along the last stretch of the road to independence, there were two problems that had to be resolved. The first was a dispute arising from the 1962 general election. Following the success in the election of Mr (now Sir) Dawda K. Jawara's People's Progressive party, the leader of the defeated United Party, Mr Pierre N'Jie, obtained a Court ruling that the electoral register used was invalid. An Order-in-Council of May 1963 from the Privy Council declared the register valid, and attempts by the United Party to get this Order-in-Council declared *ultra vires* by the High Court and Court of Appeal in London were unsuccessful.

The Gambia and Senegal

The second problem concerned the Gambia's relations with Senegal. In September 1963 a United Nations Commission of experts was appointed at the Gambia Government's request to examine and report on the future relationship between the two countries. Their report, submitted in March 1964, studied by the two governments at joint meetings in May and June 1964, and released in the latter month, described three possible forms of association:

(a) the integration of the Gambia with Senegal, which would be the most straightforward course, but would ignore the Gambia's distinctive interests and identity, and would therefore almost certainly be rejected by her electorate;

(b) a federation of Senegambia, with the federal government being given, at least initially, only subjects such as defence and foreign affairs; and

(c) an entente between the two countries, with the aim of promoting economic co-operation without creating a new political entity.

The experts gave it as their opinion that the second of these forms of association would be the most advantageous to both sides, although it described the third as the most flexible. It was this third form which was accepted by the two governments. In March 1964, President Senghor of Senegal had paid a two-day visit to Bathurst, and later announced that he and Mr (later Sir) Dawda Jawara had agreed to co-ordinate their development programmes, especially in agriculture; to improve their international communications; and to extend bi-lingualism. It was in such fields that, for the present, links between the two countries would be formed and strengthened.

The Constitutional Conference — The Gambia independent

With the validity of the 1962 general elections and the future pattern of Senegambian relations established, both the British and the Gambian governments began actively to plan for the independence of The Gambia. In July 1964 a constitutional conference was held in London, attended by representatives of all the Gambian political parties, as well as by the Governor, Sir John Paul, and representatives of the British Government. At its close it was announced that The Gambia would become independent in February 1965; but both Mr N'Jie and Mr Garba-Jahumpa (leader of the Gambia Congress Party) refused to attend the final session or sign the final communiqué, after the rejection by the conference of their request for fresh elections before independence. The two Opposition leaders explained their action on the grounds that the electorate had not given the government a mandate on the Senegambian issue, and that it was the British Privy Council, not a Gambian court, which had declared the 1962 general elections valid.

Britain agreed to continue to assist The Gambia by meeting the budget deficit of about £500,000, and by helping her to carry out the economic development programme on which The Gambia planned to spend about £4 million in the years 1964—7. The chief item was communications, others were public works, education, housing, land development, social welfare and public health. The Gambia hoped to obtain foreign loans as well as British help to meet this expenditure. In May 1964 a Gambia Currency Board was set up, as the West African Currency Board set up in 1912 was breaking up.

On February 18, 1965 The Gambia became an independent state, the twenty-first member of the Commonwealth and the thirty-seventh independent African state. On June 2, 1965 the Gambian House of Representatives adopted a resolution seeking to make The Gambia a republic within the Commonwealth on February 18, 1966, the first anniversary of independence. However, a referendum held in November 1965 failed to produce the necessary two-thirds majority for this change.

Economically The Gambia is not strong; groundnuts account for ninety per cent of its small exports, which also include beeswax, hides and skins, cotton and palm-oil. A search is being made for petroleum. The United Kingdom has promised grants of a million pounds in all for recurrent expenditure up to and including 1967, and also grants for capital expenditure. In October 1965

Independent West Africa: The Commonwealth Countries

Gambian road traffic changed over to a 'keep right' rule, to conform to the rule in Senegal.

b. SIERRA LEONE

Since April 27, 1961 Sierra Leone has been an independent sovereign state within the Commonwealth. Queen Elizabeth II is Queen of Sierra Leone and is represented by the Governor- General, Sir Henry Lightfoot-Boston, a Sierra Leonean who was formerly Speaker of the House of Representatives. The population of the country according to the 1963 census was 2,183,000 and its area is 27,924 square miles.

The first Prime Minister, Sir Milton A. S. Margai, died in April 1964. He had been leader of the government since 1954 and also leader of the Sierra Leone People's Party. He was a physician and the son of a wealthy merchant of Bonthe in the Southern Province. Originally his party was formed as a protest against the monopoly of influence by the Creoles of Freetown, but it became a national party representative of both the protectorate and the colony, and its position was further strengthened when it was joined at the time of the London Independence talks by the chief Opposition party, the People's National Party, led by Sir Milton's brother, Mr Albert Margai.

The general elections of May 1963, were keenly contested by four main political parties; the Sierra Leone People's Party, the All People's Congress led by Mr Siaka Stevens, the United People's Party and the Sierra Leone People's Independence Movement. In addition there were 116 independent candidates, out of a total of 215 candidates. In the first instance the S.L.P.P. won twenty-eight of the sixty-two directly elected seats, the A.P.C.-S.L.P.I.M. alliance twenty and Independents fourteen. Of the Independents twelve immediately joined the S.L.P.P., so Sir Henry Lightfoot-Boston, then acting Governor-General, called on Sir Milton Margai once more to form a government. In addition to the directly elected representatives there were elected twelve paramount chiefs. These were elected by the district councils from thirty candidates, one woman being among those returned. The chiefs too supported Sir Milton Margai. This election was an example of the democratic pattern Sierra Leone has been able to maintain. When Sir Milton Margai died in April 1964, the Governor-General called upon Mr Albert Margai (very soon afterwards Sir Albert Margai) to form a government.

Diplomatic and economic activity

Within four months of independence Sierra Leone imposed a ban on all trade and communications with South Africa, and on the entry into Sierra Leone of white South Africans. While being from the beginning a strong supporter of the Organization of African Unity, it has been a moderating influence among African States. It has sought close economic co-operation with neighbouring states, including the creation of a free-trade area with Guinea, Liberia and the Ivory Coast.

Economic progress since independence

Sierra Leone has made substantial economic progress since independence. It has got diamond smuggling under control, and has made taxation agreements with the Sierra Leone Selection Trust and the Diamond Corporation (Sierra Leone) to ensure that the government get more revenue from this major mineral resource. The government has also to set up its own diamond-cutting industry. Diamonds and iron are Sierra Leone's chief items of export trade. A ten-year development plan published in 1962 will cost approximately £164 million to implement, £138 million of this in the first five years, and £56 million to be found locally.

Subsistence farming remains the occupation of the bulk of the population, and farmers are being encouraged to improve their methods and co-operate to form larger farming units. The Njala University College in the Southern Province has been started to develop agricultural research and techniques. It opened in September 1964 with just over a hundred students reading agriculture, education and home economics. The College is being developed with some financial assistance from the U.S. government and with the assistance of the University of Illinois. The Sierra Leone Produce Marketing Board has with government backing embarked on a very considerable plantation development with the ultimate aim of covering over 400,000 acres, and involving the cultivation of oil palms, cocoa, rubber, citrus fruits, bananas and pineapples. Chinese help has been enlisted for experiments in rice production with the aim of producing two crops a year, and in vegetable gardening.

Sierra Leone has encouraged private investment and has stated that there is no present intention of nationalizing any industries, and that if unforeseen circumstances lead to a change of policy full compensation will be paid. At the same time foreign firms are being urged to give more responsible executive positions to Sierra Leoneans. It is hoped also to develop local industries by local investment.

The aim of Sierra Leone at home and abroad is stability, and by its policy the government has encouraged the World Bank and United States and British banks to make loans which have been guaranteed by the Sierra Leone government. A further example of initiative and enterprise has been the introduction in 1964 of a new decimal currency of leones and cents — one leone being equal to ten shillings. All banks are now licensed and under the supervision of the Bank of Sierra Leone, which, in November 1964, issued the first Sierra Leone Treasury Bills. Government Development Loans are being introduced to encourage investment by private individuals and to provide the means for the carrying out of the heavy programme of development of education, social amenities and public works.

Independent West Africa: The Commonwealth Countries
c. GHANA

The period immediately after independence was one of intense diplomatic activity in Ghana. A prominent feature of this activity was the forging of links with neighbouring African countries which had also recently become independent, particularly those with Guinea and Mali which are described in Chapter 5.

The Volta River Project
There was also considerable economic activity, particularly in connection with the Volta River Project. Independence brought an intensification of negotiations for the financing of this great scheme, which had for so long been a focus of the hopes and plans of Ghana's political leaders and their economic advisers. In November 1960 an agreement was signed between the Ghana Government and a consortium called the Volta Aluminium Company (with British, Canadian and U.S. interests, led by the Kaiser Aluminium Company) to build a giant £57 million smelter to convert bauxite into aluminium, with power generated by the proposed hydro-electric plant. This agreement made the Volta River Project an economic proposition. After a United States mission had reported on the whole proposal, the U.S. government agreed to make a loan of 133 million dollars and to give investment guarantees to the Volta Aluminium Company. In March-August 1961 contracts were placed with an American firm (Kaiser's) for designs and equipment, and with an Italian consortium for the construction of the dam, the generators and the powerhouse. The cost of the Project — some £120 million it was estimated — was to be met by loans from the United States, the World Bank and Britain and by contributions from Ghana of over £30 million. In December 1961 the Volta River Authority was formed with Dr Nkrumah as chairman, and a Canadian as chief executive, and at the same time a Fuel and Power Secretariat was set up within the President's office. Eighty thousand people have to be re-settled as the lake forms behind the dam. The smelter is to start operating in 1967. Ghana's electricity needs up to 1990 will thus be met.

Other diplomatic and economic activities
For a smaller hydro-electric scheme on the Black Volta, Russian assistance was pledged in 1960. Russian technical assistance under the same agreement was to be given in many other fields including the development of nuclear power, and this close co-operation was confirmed by a visit to Ghana by President Brezhnev of the U.S.S.R. Ghana indeed was prepared to get help from any country willing to give it. Thus, an agreement was signed with the People's Republic of China; Canada in July 1961 agreed to help train Ghana's armed forces, and in May 1961 Yugoslavia undertook to build a naval base at Sekondi. To assist trade it was announced in the same month that customs barriers between Ghana and Upper

Volta would be removed. In December 1965 Ghana broke off diplomatic relations with Britain over the Rhodesian issue and in accordance with an O.A.U. Foreign Ministers' resolution.

Ghana as a socialist state

During this period too Ghana nationalized many of the services she considered essential to her economic well-being. A State Mining Corporation was formed to take over certain gold-mines, formerly British owned. In March 1961 a state agency was set up to buy most of the country's cocoa crop. About the same time the B.O.A.C. share in Ghana Airways was bought, B.O.A.C. agreeing to continue to provide technical staff and to train crews for Ghana Airways. Ghana, by owning the airline, was able to operate services, which, though not economic, would increase her prestige and help to promote African unity.

In October 1961 a State Planning Commission and a State Control Commission under Dr Nkrumah's chairmanship were set up to plan, co-ordinate and control all government development activities and foreign investment programmes. In the same month a new and powerful transmitting station was inaugurated to make Ghana's views known to the world. The policy of asserting and concentrating the authority of the State in Ghana was furthered in June 1962 by the setting up of a State Farms Corporation with assistance with seed, equipment, management and technical training for Ghanaians provided by the U.S.S.R. The farms were to grow maize, rice and pulse, and raise cattle and poultry, and were initially to extend over 6,000 acres.

The President and the armed forces

A shaking-off of dependence on outside help and at the same time an extension of presidential authority was achieved by the assumption in September 1961 by the President of direct command of the armed forces, the remaining British officers becoming advisers only. The British connection in this sphere has, however, continued, as in May 1962 an agreement was signed whereby Britain was to provide a joint services team to assist in the development of Ghana's armed forces.

Tema and the Black Star Line

One of the greatest of Ghana's economic enterprises has been the development of the new port at Tema with a new town and a new industrial area associated with it, all benefiting from the latest techniques of modern planning. Another notable enterprise is the formation of the Black Star Line, government-owned and carrying the Ghana flag to ports throughout the world. It was given a start when in March 1963 the British Treasury gave a loan of over two million pounds for two cargo ships which were to be built on Tyneside in England, where there was considerable unemployment. It was hoped that Ghana's balance of trade would be helped by her own ships carrying her exports and imports. Another innovation was the setting up of the State Diamond Marketing Board to be responsible for buying, selling and exporting all diamonds mined in Ghana. Once again U.S.S.R. help was enlisted to value the stones and train Ghanaians in the necessary skills.

Educational and social progress

In higher education the 1961—3 period was one of increasing state activity. As we have seen, in October 1961 the University College of Ghana which was founded in 1948 and was in special relationship with the University of London (whose degrees its students took), was succeeded by the University of Ghana, academically completely independent of foreign universities. At the same time the Kumasi College of Technology[1] was similarly succeeded by the Kwame Nkrumah University of Science and Technology. Two years later a University College of Science Education was added at Cape Coast, and placed in special relationship with the University of Ghana, with the special task of training science teachers for Ghana's schools.

Another sphere where the state has extended its activities is the provision of housing. The First Ghana Building Society was formed to invite subscriptions from private individuals and to make loans for the purchase or construction of homes. The Ghana Housing Corporation was established to undertake the mass construction of homes of varying types to suit family circumstances. As a result in Accra and Tema and other places well-planned housing estates and well-built homes, mostly flats, are to be seen. 10,954 such homes had been built by the Corporation by April 1963, and work is now starting on a new satellite city near Nungua on the Accra—Tema road to provide eight thousand more new houses costing £2.5 million.

Political Developments

The years following independence were years of political disquiet. Dr J. B. Danquah, the founder of the United Gold Coast Convention, who had invited Dr Nkrumah to be its first Secretary-General, stood against Dr Nkrumah in the 1960 presidential election and was defeated. This defeat was inevitable, as after Dr Nkrumah had formed the Convention People's Party, Dr Danquah was the leader of only a small group in opposition. Then, in July 1961, the Minister of Finance announced an austerity budget which introduced a compulsory saving scheme which caused much resentment. At the same time, taxes and scarcities were pushing up the cost of living and in September 1961 serious dock and railway strikes broke out in Sekondi, Takoradi, Kumasi and Accra. Much alarmed, Dr

---

[1] Since renamed the Kumasi University of Science and Technology.

Nkrumah rushed back from the U.S.S.R. to make a successful personal radio appeal to the workers to return to work, at the same time ordering stringent measures against those who refused to do so. Such strikes were quite unexpected as the various workers' and co-operative organizations were regarded as wings of the C.P.P. In October 1961 Dr Danquah and another opposition leader, Mr Joe Appiah, were arrested under the Preventive Detention Act of 1958, which gave the government the power to imprison without trial persons considered a threat to the security of the state. A special court was set up by the National Assembly to try offences against the State, and later, in November 1963, the Preventive Detention Act was extended for a further five years. That there was also trouble within the C.P.P. was revealed when the President dismissed from the Cabinet two of his closest colleagues.

The troubles seemed to have died down when in August 1962 an attempt was made on the life of Dr Nkrumah at Kulungugu on his way back through Northern Ghana from talks with President Yameogo of Upper Volta. A number of people were killed by the bomb. The National Assembly passed a private members' bill inviting Dr Nkrumah to become life President, and another calling for the establishment of a one-party state. This incident was followed by others, and in a series of bomb explosions in Accra fifteen people were killed and many injured. A state of emergency was declared in Accra and Tema, houses (including those of members of Parliament) were searched, news was censored, some newspaper correspondents were expelled, as were Dr Roseveare, Bishop of Accra, and Archbishop Patterson, Anglican Archbishop of West Africa, who at this time criticized Ghana's youth movement. Dr Roseveare was later allowed to return; Archbishop Patterson who was only on a visit to Ghana returned to Lagos.

Even after Dr Nkrumah had refused the life Presidency in October 1962 violence continued. In January 1963 a bomb exploded in the Accra Stadium soon after the President had left an official parade there, and there were again many casualties, some fatal. In the following year a security guard lost his life in warding off another attempt on the President's life by a gunman. Among the persons arrested in connection with these incidents were two former Cabinet ministers who were tried by the special court and acquitted in December 1963, while two other accused were sentenced to death. The President dismissed the Chief Justice, Sir Arku Korsah, who had presided over the special court, and asked for, and was given, powers to annul the decisions of the special court. The Commissioner of Police and nine of his officers were also dismissed, as well as three other judges. The two Cabinet ministers, Mr Ako Adjei and Mr Adamafio, and three others were put up for trial again and sentenced to death for conspiracy to treason. Their sentences were commuted in March 1964 to twenty years' imprisonment. Dr Danquah, who was again imprisoned under the Preventive Detention Act in January 1963, died in prison in February 1965.

Independent West Africa: The Commonwealth Countries

Ghana becomes a one-party state

In January 1964 a referendum was held on the question whether Ghana should become a one-party state, and whether the President should be given power to dismiss judges. The results announced were that 96.5% of the electorate had ex pressed an opinion, and 99.9% of those doing so had approved the proposed changes. On February 21, 1964, Ghana became a one-party state, the President having approved an Act passed that day by the National Assembly giving legal effect to the proposals in the referendum. The party colours of red, white and green, with the black star in the central band, became the national flag. A three-man presidential commission was set up to assume the President's powers in the event of his death, resignation, absence from the country, or incapacity. In June 1965 all 198 C.P.P. candidates were returned unopposed in general elections, as was Dr Nkrumah to the Presidency.

Dr Nkrumah dismissed—February 24, 1966

Two years after the measures of February 21, 1964, the world was startled to hear that the Army and police had taken over power in Ghana. A National Liberation Committee was set up, headed by Major-General J. A. Ankrah. Dr Nkrumah and his ministers were dismissed, the Constitution and Parliament were suspended and the Convention People's Party was abolished. Dr Nkrumah was at the time on a visit to China. The new government declared its intention to introduce a new constitution as soon as possible. A number of political detainees were immediately released. One of the earliest actions of the new government was to restore full diplomatic relations with Great Britain; these had been broken off because of the Rhodesia crisis.

d. NIGERIA

Nigeria is West Africa's largest nation, with an area of 356,669 square miles and a population of 55,653,821. The story of Nigeria, in the years since she became independent in October 1960, resembles closely that of her neighbours in diplomatic activity, the quest for foreign assistance, political restlessness and economic activity.

Diplomatic activity after independence

In the months following independence Nigeria broke off diplomatic relations with France, following France's explosion for the third time of a nuclear device in the Sahara, and placed a ban on French shipping and aircraft (January 1961). It was, however, found that this action adversely affected the development programmes of Dahomey, Niger and Chad which imported certain goods through Nigerian ports. After discussion with her neighbours at the Monrovia Conference in May 1961, Nigeria lifted the ban. Diplomatic relations with France were resumed in October 1965. At this time a ban was placed on trade with South Africa, and in April 1961 diplomatic relations were established with the U.S.S.R. and ambassadors were exchanged.

The Cameroons

In February 1961, in plebiscites supervised by the United Nations, the Southern Cameroons chose to join the Federal Republic of Cameroun, and the Northern Cameroons chose to join the Federation of Nigeria. On June 1, 1961 the British Administrator of the Northern Cameroons formally handed over to the Federal Prime Minister of Nigeria documents transferring to Nigeria sovereignty over what now became the Sardauna Province of the Northern Region.

Economic aid from the United Kingdom and U.S.A.

Later in the year 1961 Nigeria benefited from substantial aid from the United Kingdom and the United States. The former gave £5 million to assist Nigerian higher education. A teacher training college was to be built in each region, technical institutions in the Eastern and Western Regions and a University in the North. The United Kingdom was to provide technical and educational experts to assist in these developments. The United States, after sending two economic missions, declared its intention of making grants and loans totalling 225 million dollars to support Nigeria's five-year development plan.

The 1961 elections

In 1961 there were two important elections. The first direct elections were held in May in the North, for a Northern House of Assembly increased in size from 131 to 170 elected seats. The Northern People's Congress led by Alhaji Sir Ahmadu Bello, Sardauna of Sokoto, was returned to power with 160 seats, the Action Group winning nine and the N.C.N.C. one. For the November 1961 elections in the East the House of Assembly was enlarged from 94 to 146. Of these the N.C.N.C., which had been in power in the East for eleven years, won 106, the Action Group fifteen, Independents twenty and the Dynamic Party five. Dr Michael Okpara led the new government.

The Anglo-Nigerian Defence Agreement ended

1962 began with the abrogation of the Anglo-Nigerian Defence Agreement which had been signed at independence and had been criticized as infringing Nigerian sovereignty. Thus, it seemed, one of the last vestiges of British power in Nigeria was removed.

Grave political crisis in the Western Region — 1962

A serious event at the end of 1962 was the virtual collapse of public order in the West. The ruling Action Group split into a faction led by Chief S. L. Akintola who formed a new United People's Party in coalition with the N.C.N.C., and the main bloc of the A.G. led by Chief Awolowo, the leader of the Opposition in the Federal Parliament. The political crisis was followed by financial difficulties and the Federal Government had to intervene to pay the Western Region government's employee's salaries and wages. The Federal Government declared a state of emergency in the West, and the Federal Prime Minister appointed a Commission of Inquiry consisting of one man — Mr Justice Coker — to look into the operations since 1954 of six Western public corporations. In December the state of emergency was ended. The Commissioner in his report criticized Chief Awolowo while exonerating Chief Akintola. He recommended that the Western Region Marketing Board should take over the National Investment and Properties Company which he held was the root of the Western Region's financial troubles, and that over £4 million should be recovered from the Action Group. The Federal government accepted these recommendations, and in March 1963 the Western Region government, now headed by Chief Akintola with a coalition of U.P.P. and N.C.N.C. behind him, announced that it would require all the N.I.P.C.'s property in the Region to pay that company's £7 million debt to the Western Region Marketing Board. Chief Awolowo, with thirty others, was charged with conspiracy to treason by the Federal authorities. In September 1963 he was found guilty with nineteen other A.G. members and prison sentences ranging from two to fifteen years were imposed. Chief Awolowo received a sentence of ten years and his deputy, Chief Enahoro, who had been deported from Britain at Nigeria's request, was sentenced to fifteen years' imprisonment.

Social and economic progress in 1962

The year 1962 also saw very important social and economic developments. The various government departments put forward their development programmes which the Governor-General, Dr Nnamdi Azikiwe, outlined in the speech from the Throne. The estimated cost was over £676 million of which roughly two-thirds was to be spent by the Federation, £99 million by the West and £75 million by the East. Among the main sectors of the programmes were primary production (13.4%), trade and industry (13.3%), education (10.3%) and administration (a very small proportion — 7 %). Nigeria herself, it was proposed, should bear much of the cost (£259 million). Seeing the country so willing to help itself, the United Kingdom, the United States, West Germany and the World Bank showed themselves willing to assist in the development of Nigeria's ports and railways, and great natural potentialities.

In 1962 a number of important federal projects were set in motion. In June the Provisional Council of the University of Lagos, Nigeria's fifth university, was inaugurated. The university would be sited at Yaba, and would have faculties of medicine, law, economics, business, science, arts and engineering. In August the Niger Dams Authority was set up, its primary responsibility being the proposed great new Kainji Dam and hydro-electric project. In September an agreement was reached by which Nigerian External Telecommunications, in which the Nigerian Government was to have a controlling interest, was to take over, on January 1, 1963, the assets and services in Nigeria of the British-owned Cable and Wireless Company.

On the labour front in November 1962 the Federal Government recognized the United Labour Congress of Nigeria which is affiliated to the International Confederation of Free Trade Unions. In January 1965 the unions in the United Labour Congress joined with the Nigerian Workers' Council to form a new organization, the Trade Unions Supreme Council.

Economic progress in 1963

The pattern of activity in the diplomatic, economic and constitutional fields was continued in 1963. An agreement was signed in February with the Cameroun Republic covering immigration, technical co-operation and trade. In March—July a trade agreement with the U.S.S.R. was finalized. This agreement provided for mutual most-favoured-nation treatment, Nigeria sending groundnuts, groundnut oil, palm kernels, palm oil, cocoa, cotton, rubber, timber, citrus fruits and tin to the Soviet Union, and receiving cars, tractors, farm machinery, newsprint, chemical products, cotton and rayon piece goods, tools and hardware from her. In June Britain announced another loan to Nigeria, this time of £1,200,000 to the Railway Corporation to buy British steel rails and accessories. The loan was repayable over twenty years at current interest rates.

Constitutional issues and their solutions in 1963
The census

The first major constitutional issue to arise during the year was that of the census, which had been taken in May 1962, and whose results were rejected in February 1963 because, it was announced after a meeting between the Federal Prime Minister and Regional Premiers, there had been a loss of confidence in their validity. The Prime Minister and Regional Premiers assumed responsibility for a new census to be held later in the year. This was in fact held in November, when 200,000 enumerators and 10,000 inspectors covered the whole country, watched by a United Nations advisory team. The results, announced in February 1964, were as follows:

North	29,777,986
East	12,388,646
West	10,278,506
Mid-West	2,533,331
Lagos	675,352
Total	55,653,821

Independent West Africa: The Commonwealth Countries

The constitutional significance of the figures was to give the North a controlling proportion of seats in the Federal House of Representatives. The Eastern Premier rejected these figures, but in June 1964 the Federal Supreme Court refused to entertain an action by the Eastern Region Government aimed at restraining the Federal Government from using the figures for deciding the boundaries of constituencies and allocating grants.

The Mid-West region

The second major constitutional issue of 1963 was the creation of a Mid-West Region. In February all parties agreed to support this proposal. In July a referendum in the Benin and Delta provinces of the West approved the move by an 89% majority, but at this time the Action Group changed its mind and opposed the move. In August the Federal House approved the Mid-West Region (Transitional Provisions) Bill, and Chief Denis Osadebay, President of the Senate, became the temporary administrator until a representative government took office in January 1964.

The crisis in the West

The third major constitutional problem was in the West where, following the split in the Action Group, the Governor tried to dismiss Chief Akintola as Premier. His action was annulled in the Supreme Court but upheld in the Privy Council, whereupon the Federal Parliament ratified an amendment of the Western Nigerian Constitution enacted by the Western Regional Parliament making legal Chief Akintola's position as Premier.

The establishment of the Republic

The final and most important constitutional development of 1963 was the establishment of a Republic. Following an all- party constitutional conference in Lagos in July, proposals for the change were agreed upon. They would be such as to involve the minimum changes in the country's political institutions, the key change being the replacement of the Governor-General by a constitutional President as Head of State. The only important additional power conferred on the President and not held by the Governor-General was that of appointing judges; but even this power he would have to exercise on the advice of the Prime Minister. Appeals to the Privy Council were abolished. The Republican Constitution Bill was passed by both Federal Houses in September, and the Federation became Republic on October 1, 1963 with Dr Azikiwe as the first President.

Economic activity in 1964

1964 began with considerable economic activity and ended with a serious political crisis. In January the International Finance Corporation (affiliated to the

World Bank) joined American, European, Japanese and Nigerian interests to set up the Nigerian Industrial Development Bank to finance industrial and mining operations. In February the £68 million contract for the building of the Kainji Dam on the Niger was awarded to the Italian Impresit consortium which was concerned with the building of the Volta and Kariba dams and others of similar magnitude. Foreign loans from the World Bank, and from a number of countries, in the latter cases to be spent on goods and services from the creditor countries, showed the wide interest in Nigerian development and confidence in its stability.

The successful search for oil

For many years another great economic enterprise had been in progress in Nigeria, especially in Eastern Nigeria. As early as 1937 the search for oil had been begun by Shell d'Arcy (now Shell B.P.) in its concession which at first covered most of the country but was later confined to 40,000 square miles, mostly in the Niger Delta area. Economic quantities were found in 1956 after years of exploration at Oloibiri in Yenagoa Province forty-five miles from Port Harcourt, from which the first shipment was made in 1958. By 1958 Shell B.P. had spent more than £60 million in its search and by 1962 this had been raised to £70 million. It would seem that the money has been well spent both from the country's and from the Company's point of view, for so rapid has been recent development that it is expected that in 1965 production will reach ten million tons, the figure originally set for 1970. Under the Petroleum Profits Tax Ordinance of 1959, the company and the Federal Government share profits equally. Shell B.P. have had to negotiate new leases, and these now cover only 16,300 square miles; the rest of the Shell B.P.'s former area has gone to other companies. The government's share of royalties and rentals is distributed thus — 50 per cent to the Region where the oil was found; 20 per cent to the Federal government and the remaining 30 per cent to the regional governments according to population. The Federation, and particularly the Eastern Region, has also benefited by the establishment of the vast refinery at Port Harcourt, and by the development of Port Harcourt itself. Indeed the whole position of the Eastern Region and its relations with its partners in the Federation have undergone a considerable change.

It is not only in the Eastern Region that oil has been found. Economic quantities of oil are expected in 1965 from Shell B.P.'s leases in the Mid-West. A new 140-mile pipeline will carry the oil from Ughelli to Bonny in the East, the ports further west being unsuited to the shipping of oil.

An important development in 1961 was the extension of the search for oil offshore. Shell B.P., Nigerian Gulf Oil, California Asiatic Oil Co., Mobil Exploration and Tennessee Nigeria Inc. each took one or more of twelve huge sectors of a thousand square miles each of sea off Nigeria's coast, and paid the Federal Government a total of £5 million for the right to search the bed for oil.

Early in 1965 the first off-shore crude oil began to flow towards the markets from Nigerian Gulf Oil's Okan sector.

1964—5 political crises

During 1964 considerable political tension gradually built up, one symptom of which was the passing in September 1964 of the Newspaper (Amendment) Act of September 1964 which imposed a penalty of £500 or one to three years' imprisonment for the publication of reports known to be false. The tension rose as the elections for the Federal House of Representatives approached. In December 1964 the Federal House was dissolved and elections for 312 seats were held (167 in the North, 70 in the East, 57 in the West, 14 in the Mid-West and 4 in Lagos). These elections were contested by two main alliances of political parties. The first, the Nigerian National Alliance, included the Northern People's Congress of Sir Ahmadu Bello, the Northern Premier; the Nigerian National Democratic Party led by Chief Akintola, the Western Premier; the Mid Democratic Front which was in opposition in the Mid-West Assembly; the Lagos State United Front; and a number of small parties. The second grouping was the United Progressive Grand Alliance led by Dr Okpara, Premier of the East. It comprised his party, the N.C.N.C., which was in power in the Mid-West as well as the East; the Action Group of Chief Awolowo, led by his deputy Alhaji Adegbenro; the Nigerian Elements Progressive Union (N.E.P.U.) which was in opposition in the North under the leadership of Alhaji Aminu Kano; and a number of smaller parties.

The U.P.G.A. boycotted the elections, alleging irregularities and atrocities. The Premier of the North and West refused to attend a meeting called by the President of the Federation to discuss the situation. The result of the elections, in which it was said only four million of fifteen million possible votes were cast, gave the N.N.A. 198 seats (162 of which were won by the N.P.C. in the North and 36 by the N.N.D.P. in the West). In the Mid West the N.C.N.C. won nine of the fourteen seats. The East virtually took no part in the election. At first the U.P.G.A. announced that it would not recognize the new government, and was ready to divide the Federation's assets. But then the President called on Alhaji Sir Abubakar Tafawa Balewa to form a 'broad-based' government, and the differences which had arisen between these two leaders were resolved, everyone agreeing to give the new government a fair trial, pending the holding of supplementary elections in the East and in Lagos. These were held in March 1965 when the U.P.G.A. won all fifty-one contested seats in the East (the other nineteen returned U.P.G.A. candidates unopposed). The leaders of two small parties, the Dynamic Party and the Socialist Workers' and Farmers' Party, Dr Chike Obi and Dr Tunji Otegbeye respectively, were defeated. Thus the final state of the parties after the elections was N.N.A. 198 and U.P.G.A. 108; with five independents and one vacant seat. A broad-based government including both groups was formed by Sir Abubakar.

That Nigeria's political problems were still acute has been shown during the summer of 1965 by the disorders occurring during the elections in the Western Region, by rumours of possible secession and by a powerful resurgence of tribalism.

In January 1966 Sir Abubakar Tafawa Balewa presided over a Conference in Lagos of Commonwealth Prime Ministers. It was the first time such a conference had been held away from London, and Sir Abubakar had taken the initiative in summoning it in an attempt to solve the Rhodesia problem. In the Commonwealth and internationally the reputation of the Federal Prime Minister seemed to stand high.

The Army takes over—January 15, 1966

Little effective action was, however, taken to solve the grave internal problems, especially in the West, and on January 15, 1966, only a few days after the end of the Commonwealth Prime Ministers' Conference, a group of young Army officers led a revolution. Among those killed were Sir Ahmadu Bello, Sardauna of Sokoto, the Northern Premier, Chief S. L. Akintola, the Western Premier, and the Federal Prime Minister, Sir Abubakar Tafawa Balewa. Major-General Aguiyi-Ironsi, the Army Commander, took over the administration. Law and order were quickly established and military governors were appointed to the Regions. Pending the drawing up of a new constitution, the existing constitution was suspended.

8
Independent West Africa: The French-speaking Countries

Federal Republic of Cameroun
The former French-administered trust territory became independent on January 1, 1960, and President Ahidjo began a five-year term as President in April 1960. In February 1961 plebiscites supervised by the United Nations were held in the British-administered trust territories North and South Cameroons. As a result of these the South Cameroons elected to join the Republic of Cameroun, and the North Cameroons chose to become part of the Federation of Nigeria. The latter result was at first disputed by the Republic of Cameroun, but was confirmed by the United Nations. On October 1, 1961 forty-two years of British rule ended in the South Cameroons which now became the Province of West Cameroun in the Federal Republic of Cameroun. In this way the Camerouns, partitioned in 1919, were re-united.

In the Federal Assembly East Cameroun (the former French territory) had forty seats and West Cameroun ten seats. French and English were both adopted as official languages. Mr John Foncha, the Premier of West Cameroun, became Vice-President of the Republic for the remainder of President Ahidjo's term. Whereas the Federal Assembly and the Assembly of East Cameroun are each of one chamber the Parliament of West Cameroun has a Legislative Assembly and a House of Chiefs. In both Provinces there is universal adult suffrage. In many respects Cameroun is tied economically to France. In 1961 Mr John Foncha's Kamerun National Democratic Party won general elections in West Cameroun, where Dr E. M. L. Endeley's Cameroun People's National Congress formed the Opposition. (These parties merged in 1965.) Later in 1961 President Ahidjo formed the first Federal Cabinet, with Mr Foncha as Vice-President.

Dahomey
Dahomey became independent on August 1, 1960 'and quickly made a Customs Union with Togo. In December 1960 the 'Parti Dahoméan de l'Unité', which was affiliated to the 'Rassemblement Démocratique Africain', won the elections for the Presidency, Vice-Presidency and National Assembly under the leadership of M. Hubert Maga. The main opposition party was the 'Union Démocratique Dahoméene', also formerly affiliated to the R.D.A. and under the leadership of M. Ahomadegbe.

M. Maga was installed as President and M. Apithy as Vice-President. In May 1961 the U.D.D. was dissolved by the government and M. Ahomadegbe and other leaders arrested on a charge of conspiracy to murder the President. In November 1962 M. Ahomadegbe, having confessed his guilt, was released.

During this period of political unrest, economic and technical agreements were made with West Germany and Israel, and in July 1962 a convention was made with Nigeria for common customs tariffs and ports. Vice-President Apithy paid a visit to the U.S.S.R. and it was agreed that Dahomey should exchange ambassadors with the Soviet Union. Dahomey's chief trade relations, however, continued to be with France and she remained dependent on France for assistance with her budget and for development aid.

1963 and 1964 were also years of considerable unrest in Dahomey. As a result of demonstrations the President dismissed the Cabinet and appointed a provisional government of three, himself, M. Apithy and M. Ahomadegbe. This did not prove to be the solution and in October 1963 the President was forced to resign, and a provisional government was formed under Colonel Christopher Soglo, the commander of the very small Dahomeyan army. In December 1963 a referendum on a new constitution led to the election in January 1964 of M. Apithy as President and M. Ahomadegbe as Vice-President and Head of Government. This uneasy partnership was unsuccessful and in November 1965 Colonel Soglo intervened again and forced the resignations of both men. In December 1965 further failures on the part of the politicians forced Colonel Soglo to take power himself once more.

At this time there was also trouble with the neighbouring Niger state over an island called Lété in the River Niger which was claimed by both countries. In December 1963 some Dahomeyans were expelled by Niger and Colonel Soglo retaliated by cutting road and rail communications. However, the 'Union Africaine et Malgache' brought about a reconciliation and a settlement of differences followed.

Unemployment, especially among the educated classes who previously found employment in other parts of West Africa, is a serious factor in unrest in Dahomey which with its long and narrow shape (a coast-line of seventy-seven miles and a depth of 415 miles) has the highest population density in West Africa, forty-five per square mile. The total population is over two million and the area 44,290 square miles.

Guinea

In September 1958, when the French constitutional referendum was held, Guinea alone of France's African territories at this stage voted to become a fully independent republic forthwith rather than remain as a self-governing country within the French community. French aid of all kinds, administrative, economic, technical and military, was at once withdrawn and Guinea was left on her own.

Independent West Africa: The French-Speaking Countries

Contrary to expectations she did not collapse, but under the leadership of M. Sékou Touré consolidated her position as an independent state. Many of Guinea's post-independence developments have resembled those of Ghana to whom she was indebted for financial assistance in the early difficult days. The general tendency, as in Ghana, has been for more and more centralization of authority in both political and economic fields. M. Sékou Touré became President and Prime Minister of the Republic of Guinea on October 2, 1958. In November 1959 a new constitution was adopted by the Assembly and under it M. Sékou Touré, the only candidate, was elected, by direct popular vote, President and head of the Government and armed forces, for a term of office of seven years.

From the beginning the first diplomatic moves were to seek economic assistance from Communist countries. In 1960 agreements were signed with the People's Republic of China for loans and technical assistance. In February 1961 President Brezhnev of the U.S.S.R. visited Guinea, and in January 1964 Mr Chou En-Lai, Prime Minister of the People's Republic of China, also paid an official visit. The strong socialist trend in the State was shown by the nationalization of electricity and water undertakings in January 1961 (with compensation to the French shareholders); by the taking over of diamond-mining concerns in March 1961; by the nationalization of the largest private transport concern in Guinea in August 1961, and by the taking over of the Canadian Aluminium Ltd, and the closure of private banks and insurance companies early in 1962. On the other hand companies working the iron deposits, and Fria, an American and European Consortium, were allowed to continue operations.

In August 1961 the Roman Catholic Archbishop of Conakry, Mgr Gerard de Milleville, like his Anglican counterpart in Accra, was expelled. He had protested in a pastoral letter against a decision by the ruling 'Parti Démocratique' that all private schools should be taken over by the state, and against a statement by the President that all churches should be national. He was asked by the government to leave voluntarily, and when he refused he was deported. The President then declared that all future Catholic prelates must be African, and in May 1962 Mgr Tchidimbo was installed the first Guinean Archbishop of Conakry.

A feature of the development of Guinea has been the strong Marxist inclination of the political leaders and of the government policy. This has been coupled with an intense interest in African history, languages and culture. There has also been a strong desire to throw off all traces of colonialism. This, however, has not led to the replacing of French as the language of instruction or of the French system of laws and justice. Nor have cultural links with France been broken. Indeed since the end of the Algerian War relations with France and the West have improved. Without sacrificing the advantages of assistance from Communist countries, Guinea has recently encouraged private investment and joined the World Bank and the International Monetary Fund. At the same time President Touré has worked with great energy for the Organization of African

Unity established in Addis Ababa in May 1963. In November 1965 the government announced the discovery of a plot against the State, and accused France, the Ivory Coast and Mr Tshombe, former Premier of the Congo, of supporting it. As a result, France and Guinea severed diplomatic relations.

The Ivory Coast

The dominating figure in the early years of the existence of the Ivory Coast as an independent state has been M. Felix Houphouet-Boigny, the founder in 1946 of the Rassemblement Démocratique Africain. At first the ally of the French Communist Party, he later changed course and followed a policy of Franco-African co-operation and free enterprise in economic development. He was a member of the French Government from 1956 to 1959, strongly supporting the French Community until Mali was granted independence in June 1960. The Ivory Coast became independent on August 7, 1960 and in November 1960 M. Houphouet-Boigny was elected President for five years by universal adult suffrage. At the same time his party, the 'Parti Démocratique de la Côte d'Ivoire', won all seventy seats in the National Assembly without opposition. In addition to Ivory Coasters, the voting list included 5,000 Frenchmen and 600,000 Africans born outside the Ivory Coast. It was the initiative of M. Houphouet-Boigny that led in 1961 to the formation of the Union Africaine et Malgache and to the adoption of its principles — the maintenance of national sovereignty, non-interference in the internal affairs of member states, and a limitation on the powers of the organization's secretary-general.

In May 1962 a co-operation agreement between Israel and the Ivory Coast was signed for the establishment of a military-agricultural youth corps in the Ivory Coast on the Israeli model, and later a more extensive treaty of friendship and cultural and technical co-operation was signed during a state visit by Houphouet-Boigny to Israel. Relations with Guinea and Mali, at first strained because of the fact that President Houphouet Boigny was much more pro-French in his foreign policy than either President Touré or President Keita, improved somewhat after January 1962; and in October 1962 the three Presidents, all former leaders of the 'Rassemblement Démocratique Africain', met in Conakry. Their role in forming a larger association of French-speaking and later English-speaking African states has been described in Chapter 5.

In spite of marked economic progress, the Ivory Coast has not escaped political unrest. The first serious disturbances were in January 1963 when a security court was set up, and there were widespread arrests of persons accused of plotting against the government. For these the Vice-President, M. Philippe Yace, blamed Communist subversion. The President dismissed three ministers, all connected with the Youth Movement in his own party and with the Union of Ivory Coast students in France. In April 1963 eighty-five persons were charged before the State Security Court with conspiracy to treason, sixty-four were found guilty, thirteen (including the former Health Minister) were sentenced to death and others to terms of imprisonment ranging from five years to life. There were further plots later in 1963, and in 1964 the President disclosed that M. Ernest Boka, a former Cabinet Minister and President of the Supreme Court, had committed suicide after arrest on suspicion of implication in yet another plot. Most of the discontent was among intellectuals and students who looked for a more revolutionary policy comparable in dynamism with that of Ghana or Guinea. In an attempt at control of the young intellectuals, it was announced that as from the beginning of 1964 all Ivory Coast students at home and overseas must join the government-approved and Abidjan-based Union of Students.

The high esteem in which the President is held abroad was shown on his goodwill tours of Ethiopia and the United Arab Republic, and by his close relations with France and a number of African countries formerly French. Indeed his Francophile policy has been one of the causes of internal unrest. The economy of the Ivory Coast is expanding more rapidly than that of any other French-speaking African country. With a prosperous agriculture, producing cocoa and palm products, with valuable mineral deposits, including diamonds and manganese, and with substantial investment of French capital and assistance in the form of loans and gifts, the prospects of the Ivory Coast are bright. Abidjan itself is a wealthy — and expensive — city and one of the most modern and one of the busiest of African ports. In September 1965, outside Abidjan, an oil refinery with a capacity of 700,000 tons of crude oil a year went into production, a month ahead of schedule.

Mali

Mali, an independent republic, covers a vast area approaching half a million square miles and has a population of some four and a half millions. In 1959, when it was known as the French Soudan, it belonged to the French Community but became independent of the community in September 1960. For a short time it was joined in federation with neighbouring Senegal (January 1959—August 1960). M. Modibo Keita was elected first Head of State in 1959 and has since been confirmed as President of the Republic of Mali. The one political party, the Union Soudanaise-Rassemblement Démocratique Africain (U.S.-R.D.A.) is deeply influenced by Marxist ideas and a desire to cast off all traces of colonial rule, while developing Mali's sense of nationhood by strict party discipline. Though it has developed close relations in economic and technical matters with the U.S.S.R., Czechoslovakia, the People's Republic of China and Yugoslavia, it has also received help from France and the United States, and in general follows a policy of non-alignment. In keeping with this policy, Mali asked France in January 1961 to withdraw her troops from bases in Mali. Another aspect of Mali policy was the decision at the Casablanca Conference of December 1960 to set up a Ghana-Guinea-Mali Union, but the scheme was never effectively carried out.

In 1961 Mali announced a substantial credit of nearly £6 million from the United Arab Republic following a visit of President Keita to that country. In the latter part of 1963 and early 1964 agreements for technical, scientific and cultural co-operation were signed with Poland, with the People's Republic of China whose Premier Mr Chou En-Lai visited the Mali capital, Bamako, in January 1964, and with the U.S.S.R., President Keita having visited Moscow in May 1962. The bi-lateral nature of Mali's policy was, however, shown by the co-operation and cultural agreements with France, the former colonial power, one of the agreements specifying that Mali should remain in the franc area. Another development in 1963 was a treaty for mutual co-operation and friendship with the Ivory Coast, with whom there had been considerable differences about foreign policy.

Mali had her full share of political unrest during these years. In July 1962 demonstrations took place in Bamako against the new Mali franc, and in September that year ninety-one persons, including two opposition politicians who had once been members of the French Government, MM. Hammadou Dicko and Fily Dabo, were tried for treason by a 'People's Court'. Seventy-six of the accused were found guilty, and MM. Dicko and Dabo were amongst three sentenced to death the others being sentenced to hard labour. President Keita, however, commuted the death sentences to hard labour in October 1962.

In April 1964 general elections were held in Mali for the eighty-seat National Assembly. There was a single list of candidates, all nominated by the ruling 'Union Soudanaise', which had also held all the seats in the former Assembly. An announcement stated that all the valid votes were in favour of the list. Another interesting feature of the election was that, as a gesture towards African unity, Mali, like the Ivory Coast, allowed all citizens of other African countries resident in Mali to vote.

In the economic field the position of Mali has been difficult. It is a poor country with many social as well as economic problems. The vast majority of the population are subsistence farmers or pastoralists. Much help from abroad is necessary to develop mineral resources which include bauxite and manganese. Mali cannot do without French cultural as well as economic help — French remains the official language; nor can she do without credits and technical assistance from the West as well as from China and the U.S.S.R.

Niger

This vast country of 459,000 square miles has a population of between two and a half and three millions. Only two per cent of its area has sufficient water to allow regular cultivation. Since it became independent in August 1960, Niger has maintained very close relations with France and has cultivated good relations

Independent West Africa: The French-Speaking Countries

with her neighbours, including Nigeria, Ivory Coast and Upper Volta, through which Niger's external trade must pass. In 1961 co-operation agreements were signed with France whereby French aid to Niger was to continue for five years, to aid defence, economic and social development, the staffing of the civil service and the setting up of a University. A customs union was formed with Nigeria in January 1963, and financial and technical help has been sought from the United States, Egypt and Israel and from other African states. Following the reported discovery of valuable tungsten deposits in the Air Mountains, Niger sought the co-ordination of development plans with her neighbours both to avoid harmful competition and to secure a fresh agreement regarding the harnessing of the River Niger's resources for the benefit of all countries through which it flows. By September 1963 Niger was able to produce a budget which balanced without foreign aid, and, in October 1964, she was able to take over the last French military bases and end the agreement by which a thousand French troops were stationed in the country. The French military connection is, however, well maintained by the great number of ex-servicemen or 'veterans', Niger having been one of the chief French recruiting grounds for African troops.

The dominant figure in Niger politics before and since independence has been President Hamani Diori, a French-educated Hausa and former schoolmaster. His party in 1958 won the elections against the former radical party in power, which advocated union with Guinea. M. Djibo Bakary, the leader of this party, the Sawaba, has been exiled since 1960. There have been alleged disturbances by members of this party, as a result of one of which four men were sentenced to death by a security court and publicly executed. There was an attempt to assassinate President Diori in April 1965. Niger has complained that other neighbouring states have not been so co operative in dealing with these threats as Nigeria where the Sawaba party was banned in July 1965.

Niger has been assisted not only by France but by the European Economic Community and the International Development Association. She has also had technical assistance from Israel, like a number of other West African states. With most of her neighbours her relations have been cordial but her disagreement in 1963 with Dahomey over the island of Lété in the Niger was only settled by the Heads of State of the Union Africaine et Malgache at Dakar in March 1964. Internally there are elements which look for less reliance on France and a more positive and revolutionary approach to national development.

Senegal

Senegal began its life as an independent state with the advantage of being relatively compact (area 76,084 square miles; population 3,100,000), but it had the disadvantage of being poor in natural resources. Dakar, the capital, had been the administrative capital of French West Africa. It was the chief port in West Africa, it had its own University and a large airport. The government had the advantage of a well-developed radio network, good economic planning machinery, and better road and rail communication than most other West African countries. Furthermore there were in Senegal some of West Africa's most experienced politicians, headed by the much respected M. Léopold Senghor who was elected President in September 1960, and re-elected by popular referendum for a four-year term in December 1963. In the December 1963 elections, the Union Progressiste Sénégalaise won all eighty seats — the voting being by universal adult suffrage for a four-year term.

The Senghor régime has survived two great crises. The first was the collapse of the Senegal-Soudan (Mali) Federation in August 1960. The delicately balanced arrangement whereby Soudan supplied the Prime Minister (M. Modibo Keita) and Senegal the President (M. Léopold Senghor) collapsed when it was thought that M. Keita was seeking to turn the scales decisively in favour of the Soudan. Keita was arrested and expelled, the Federation ended and the frontier between Senegal and the Soudan (now Mali) closed until June 1963, with unhappy results for both countries.

The second crisis occurred in 1962 when a split developed in the Union Progressiste Sénégalaise. There was at that time a balance of power in the Constitution between the Prime Minister (M. Mamadou Dia) and the President (M. Léopold Senghor). These two men had been closely associated in politics and by friendship for seventeen years, and there was no radical difference of principle between them. The difficulties arose from questions of their own authority, and of relations with and dependence on France. Senghor had behind him the conservative elements, Muslim and Christian, Dia was spurred on by nationalists, mostly students, especially younger Christians, who wanted more positive action. The test came in December 1962 when conflict arose between the National Assembly and Dia. Senghor supported the Assembly, as did most of the army. Dia and the commander-in-chief of the army who supported him were arrested. No shots were fired, but subsequently in May 1963 Dia was sentenced to life imprisonment and others were also imprisoned for long terms. A new constitution of March 1963 established a presidential type of government by which the President could dissolve the Assembly. The latter on the other hand was given power to impeach the President of high treason before the High Court, and the Supreme Court could adjudicate lesser issues between Assembly and President. Other powers vested in the President were that of submitting proposed legislation to a national referendum, and of assuming certain arbitrary authority in times of national emergency. The opposition parties boycotted the referendum on the constitution.

In the elections held in December 1963 already mentioned, the Opposition party, the Parti du Regroupement Africain was allowed to campaign freely. There was some violence and twelve people were killed. The opposition won no seats

Independent West Africa: The French-Speaking Countries

in the 'single-list' system whereby a vote was cast for an entire party list rather than for individual candidates.

Senegal's economy is weak. Limestone for cement and groundnuts are its chief exports. It therefore depends greatly on French assistance in the form of grants to balance its budget, subsidized markets for its groundnuts, and development aid. Although completely independent, it has, alone of the countries of former French West Africa, remained in the French Community, and France, in return for its economic help, has been allowed to maintain a large military base in Senegal. Senegal has a trade agreement with West Germany, and agreements for trade and economic and technical co-operation with the U.S.S.R.

The relations between Senegal and The Gambia have already been mentioned in the section on the latter.

Togo

Togo, the smallest of The West African states, has a population of well over one and a half million and an area of 21,850 square miles. Until it became independent in April 1960, it was administered by France as a trust territory. It was the eastern part of the former German territory of Togoland. The western half, formerly a British-administered territory, has elected to be integrated with Ghana. The official language is French. Its President is M. Nicolas Grunitzky, elected in May 1963. It has a one-chamber legislature to which each of the four major political parties contribute fourteen members, having agreed on a single list of National Unity and Reconciliation for the elections of May 1963. It has close diplomatic and economic ties with Yugoslavia, following Marshal Tito's visit in 1961, and also with Israel. There is also a customs union with Dahomey.

The dominant figure in Togo politics at the time of independence was M. Sylvanus Olympio who was elected President in April 1961 for a seven-year term, being the only candidate. During 1962 there were reports of subversive plots, and there was evidence of these in assassination attempts on M. Olympio. The President dissolved Juvento, a political union hostile to him, and its leaders, M. Grunitzky and M. Meatchi, fled. In October 1962 M. Olympio was elected leader for life of his party, Parti de L'Unité Togolaise. In January 1963, however, he was assassinated, and the two exiled leaders, M. Grunitzky and M. Meatchi, returned. M. Grunitzky formed a provisional government, dissolved the Assembly, abrogated the constitution and declared a general amnesty. The new régime was recognized at once by Ghana, Dahomey and Senegal as well as by France, but other African states, led by Guinea, deplored the violence by which it gained power. In May 1963 M. Grunitzky was elected President for five years with M. Meatchi as Vice-President. The new Assembly elected at the same time supported the new government, which was thereupon quickly recognized by other nations. A feature of the government's policy has been the establishment of close links with France both in defence and economic policy, and an agreement to confer with France on foreign policy and other matters. Togo is hampered by its limited economic possibilities, phosphate being its chief natural resource.

Upper Volta

The Upper Volta with a population of four and a half millions and an area of 105,900 square miles looks back in history to the old Mossi empire, and has made the centre of that empire, Ouagadougou, its capital. The Mossi element in the population is more than one and a half million and is viewed jealously by the other elements. The Head of State from April 1959 to January 1966 was M. Maurice Yameogo, first as Prime Minister and later as President. The ruling party, the Union Démocratique Voltaique, had all fifty seats in the National Assembly. There was, nevertheless, political discontent, chiefly among educated young Voltaics and the numerous veterans of the French army. On January 4, 1966 the Army chief of staff, Colonel Lamizana, deposed M. Yameogo and installed a military government.

In its short history as an independent state Upper Volta has attempted to work closely with Ghana, and all customs barriers between the countries were removed in 1960. It has also considered joining the Mali Federation. It was a founding member of the Union Africaine et Malgache. In spite of President Yameogo's wish to show an independent attitude, and his determination to get rid of French forces in the country, he has been unable to do without French and European Economic Community assistance. Upper Volta's economic problems may be partly solved when the valuable manganese deposits are fully worked.

The elements of discontent were given a powerful weapon when in February 1964 France was allowed to set up a satellite tracking station near Ouagadougou. On the other hand Upper Volta's trade unions are closely linked with those of Ghana. Upper Volta has, too, maintained very close relations with her French-speaking neighbours. In December 1964 the Presidents of the Ivory Coast, Niger, Mauritania and Senegal all went to Ouagadougou to celebrate the fourth anniversary of the country's independence, and to discuss their relations with the O.A.U. and other groupings of African states. The Ivory Coast and Niger went so far as to agree to establish in due course a common citizenship with Upper Volta.

A successful state visit was paid by President Yameogo to the U.S.A. in March 1965. Two months before this the Pope had created an Upper Volta citizen a Cardinal — the first West African and second African to be so honoured. He was Paul Zoungrana, who had been Archbishop of Ouagadougou since 1960.

SUGGESTED QUESTIONS

CHAPTER 1
(1) What was the importance of *either* (a) the Gambia, or (b) Sierra Leone to the British in the nineteenth century?
(2) Show how the Creole population of Sierra Leone was made up. What part did it play in the government of the Colony?
(3) How did European nations try to enforce the ban on the transatlantic slave trade?
(4) Why was the Sierra Leone Protectorate annexed? What were the causes and results of the 1898 rising?
(5) What role did missionaries and traders play in the extension of British influence and rule in West Africa?
(6) Describe and account for the many changes in the British administration of the colonies and settlements in West Africa during the nineteenth century.
(7) What were the chief recommendations of the Select Committee of 1865? Why were they not acted upon?
(8) Why were the Asante a continual threat to the Gold Coast in the nineteenth century?
(9) Write notes on (a) the Bond of 1844, (b) the Fante Confederation, and (c) the Mankessim constitution.

CHAPTER 2
(1) Explain the decline of the Yoruba Empire.
(2) What were the causes of the prolonged civil wars in Yorubaland?
(3) What were the causes and results of the Fulani *jihad*, and what was the nature and extent of the Fulani empire?
(4) Why did the British (a) intervene in Lagos in 1851, and (b) make Lagos a Crown Colony in 1861?
(5) Describe the development of European trade in the Delta and on the Niger.
(6) Trace the events that led to the declaration of the various British protectorates in Nigeria and ultimately to the formation of British Nigeria in 1900.

CHAPTER 3
(1) Outline the history of the Gambia (including constitutional changes) in the twentieth century prior to independence.
(2) Trace the constitutional advances made in Sierra Leone in the twentieth century prior to independence.
(3) What were the objects of *(a)* the Gold Coast Aborigines' Rights Society, and *(b)* the National Congress of West Africa?
(4) Outline the constitutional changes made in the Gold Coast (Ghana) in the twentieth century prior to the winning of independence.

(5) Describe the part played by Dr Kwame Nkrumah in the winning of independence for Ghana.

CHAPTER 4
(1) Describe the part played by Sir Frederick (Lord) Lugard in the history of Nigeria.
(2) What do you understand by 'indirect rule'? Why was it more successful in Northern Nigeria than in Eastern Nigeria?
(3) Trace the main stages of constitutional development in Nigeria in the twentieth century down to the obtaining of independence.
(4) What was the importance of the part played by Dr Nnamdi Azikiwe in the events leading to the winning of independence?
(5) Describe the economic development of Nigeria in the twentieth century down to 1960.

CHAPTER 5
(1) Describe in general terms the method of government in French West Africa prior to the Second World War.
(2) Trace the beginnings of political parties in French-speaking West Africa.
(3) What do you understand by the terms (*a*) assimilation, and (*b*) association as applied to the relations of France with French West Africa?
(4) What were the objects of the French Community? Why did it break up so quickly?
(5) Give an account of the creation of the Organization of African Unity and of its progress to the present time.

CHAPTER 6
(1) Outline Liberia's early history down to the Declaration of Independence on July 26, 1847.
(2) What are the chief features of Liberia's constitution? What does it owe to the American constitution?
(3) What economic difficulties has Liberia had to face in the twentieth century?

CHAPTER 7
(1) Why has it been found impossible so far to form a federation of Senegambia?
(2) Outline the political and economic developments in Sierra Leone from the general elections of May 1963 to the present time.
(3) What do you understand by the statement 'Ghana is a socialist state"?
(4) Show how and why Ghana became a 'one-party' state.

Suggested Questions

(5) Show the importance to Ghana's economic development of the Volta River and Tema projects.
(6) What are the strong points and what are the weaknesses of the federal constitution of Nigeria?
(7) What are the reasons for the recurrent political crises in the Western region of Nigeria?
(8) Why was the Mid-West Region of Nigeria created?
(9) Give an account of (a) the educational progress, and (b) the economic progress of Nigeria since independence.

CHAPTER 8

(1) Describe the political experiences of any *one* French-speaking state of West Africa, showing whether they can be said to be typical of or different from the experience of other such states.
(2) Describe in general terms the relations of the French-speaking states of West Africa with France since independence.
(3) How real a tie is French culture and the French language for the French-speaking countries of West Africa?
(4) Describe the economic development since independence of any *one* state of French-speaking West Africa, showing the nature and source of foreign assistance.
(5) What attempts have been made at unions or federations in French-speaking West Africa since independence? How successful have they been?

TIME CHART

DATE	THE GAMBIA	SIERRA LEONE	GHANA	NIGERIA
1800	British attacked and took Goree and drove French from Albreda	Maroons arrived in Freetown and foiled Nova Scotian revolt		Estimated 18,000 Ibo being sold as slaves every year
1801		War between Temne and colony began	Osei Bonsu succeeded Osei Kwame as Asantehene about now	Katsina now leading military and commercial state in the north
1802				Yuni succeeded Nafata as King of Gobir
1804				Fulani Jihad started in the north by Usman dan Fodio at Battle of Tabkin Kwatto
			[*Denmark declared slave trade illegal*	
1806		War between Temne and colony ended	Asante beat Fante at Battle of Abora. British recognized Ashanti rulers of Fante	
1807		Temne abandoned north shore of peninsula to colonists		
			[*Britain declared slave trade illegal*	

Time Chart

DATE	THE GAMBIA	SIERRA LEONE	GHANA	NIGERIA
1808		S.L. declared a Crown Colony		Mai ruler fled from Bornu Ngazargamu before Fulani attack
			[*Britain importing 200 tons of palm oil from W. Africa*	
1809				El Kanemi saved Bornu
			[*U.S.A. declared slave trade illegal*	
1811		Rev. George Warren arrived as a missionary	Asante, Ga and Elmina defeated Fante, Akim and Akwapim	Fulani held Ngazargamu briefly
1812		Governor's Council given first non-official member	Akwapim took Dutch Apam and British Tantamkweri	
1813			[*Sweden declared slave trade illegal*	
1814		The Christian Institution founded at Leicester by C.M.S.	Asante again defeated Akim and Akwapim but lost Ga ally	
			[*Holland declared slave trade illegal*	
1815	Albreda returned to France	Susu returned Port Loko to Temne		
			[*End of Napoleonic Wars. France banned slave trade*	
1816	King of Kombo 'gave' Banjol (St Mary's) Island to British in return for protection	Regent Church founded by C.M.S.	Philip Quacoe died. Asante masters of Fante coastline	
			[*American Colonization Society formed. Spain banned slave trade*	

West Africa in History

DATE	THE GAMBIA	SIERRA LEONE	GHANA	NIGERIA
1817	Charles MacCarthy became Governor of Gambia, S.L. and G.C.		British made treaty of friendship with Asantehene. Hutchinson appointed Resident	Ilorin helped by Fulani to break away from Oyo
			[*Portugal banned slave trade*]	
1818	Bathurst named and became capital	Americans tried to resettle freed slaves in Sherbro		Break-up of Yoruba empire of Oyo in progress
			[*American Colonization Society sent freed slaves to settle in Sherbro*]	
1819	Governor's Council set up		British Consul Dupuis joined Resident in Kumasi, and quarrelled with Governor Hope Smith at Cape Coast	
1820	Goree abandoned by British to French			
1821	First missionaries came. Gambia now a Crown Colony	Governor of S.L. also administered Gambia and G.C.	Factories at 10 places handed by British Co. to Br. Governor MacCarthy	Oyo's power finally collapsed Yoruba wars began
1822	Timber first exported	Sherbro settlers moved to Monrovia and founded Liberia		
			[*Liberia founded by settlers from Sherbro*]	

142

Time Chart

DATE	THE GAMBIA	SIERRA LEONE	GHANA	NIGERIA
1823	French Sisters of Charity started work in Bathurst			
1824	MacCarthy Island now 'British' in return for protection	G.C. separated from S.L.	MacCarthy killed by Asante at Nsamankow; Osei Bonsu died; Osei Yaw Akoto became Asantehene	
1825	87 of 108 British troops died here		Asante at height of their power after defeat of British and Denkyera at Efutu	
1826	King of Barra 'ceded' sovereignty to British. 1,800 people living in Bathurst		British-built alliance of Fanti, Ga, Akim and Denkyera defeated Asante at Dodowa	
1827	Gambia Commandant allowed to correspond direct with London	Christian Institution became Fourah Bay College		
1828	Brikama and Fattatenda claimed by British		Basel missionaries arrived in Christiansborg. British Government handed forts to Committee of Merchants	
1829	Lt.-Governor allowed to communicate direct with London			

West Africa in History

DATE	THE GAMBIA	SIERRA LEONE	GHANA	NIGERIA
1830	Groundnuts first exported		Maclean became Governor, appointed by Merchants	Fulani Jihad ended in success in the north
1831			Maclean signed agreement with Asante, recognizing independence of Denkyera and Assin	Fulani controlled Ilorin directly
1832				Ibadan and Abeokuta now expanding rapidly
1834	Wesleyan Church began work in Bathurst. Deer Island fell under British rule			
1835			Wesleyans began work at Cape Coast; Asante and Juaben reconciled	
1837				Fulani Emir of Ilorin destroyed old Oyo (Katunga)
1838			Kwaku Dua succeeded Osei Yaw Akoto as Asantehene	New Oyo capital founded at Ago Oja
1839			Asante re-opened war against Assin, Akim and Denkyera	

Time Chart

DATE	THE GAMBIA	SIERRA LEONE	GHANA	NIGERIA
1840	Kombo 'acquired' by British for liberated Africans	First mission to Temne opened by C.M.S. at Magbele		Fulani of Ilorin defeated by Ibadan at Oshogbo
1841	King of Kataba signed treaty of protection with British	Temne defeated Loko at Kasona		British signed first treaty for the suppression of the slave trade with King Pepple of Bonny
1842	Marabout-Soninke wars	Americans opened mission to Mende on River Jong		Christian missionaries arriving in large numbers
1843	Wuli and Bondu war. Gambia separated administratively from S.L.	Riots at Waterloo amongst liberated Africans. Committee set up to represent all people	British Government resumed administration. Hill succeeded Maclean as Governor	
1844	Gambia given Executive and Legislative Councils		British Crown Colony of the G.C. 'created' by Bond	Ibadan at war with Ijaye (until 1846)
1845		First boys' grammar school in W.A. opened by C.M.S. in Freetown		
1846				Sef rulers expelled from Bornu by Omar
1847			Bremen missionaries started work	

[*Liberia became independent*

145

DATE	THE GAMBIA	SIERRA LEONE	GHANA	NIGERIA
1848	Groundnuts overtook beeswax as most valuable export			
1849	Sisters from Cluny arrived to work as missionaries	First girls' grammar school in W.A. opened by C.M.S. in Freetown		Beecroft was appointed British consul over Bights of Benin and Biafra
1850	British raided Kunnong in revenge for attacks on Governor's expedition		5 Danish forts bought by British	Kosoko King of Lagos hostile to British

[*Transatlantic slave trade virtually ceased*

1851				Abeokuta at war with Dahomey; Ibadan with Ilesha (until 1854)
1852	Gambia included in Diocese of S.L.	Diocese of S.L. created	Poll tax levied, and provoked unsuccessful revolt near Accra	Puppet Akitoye was made King of Lagos, now a British protectorate

[*Regular mail-boat service linked Britain and W.A.*

1853				King Pepple of Bonny exiled to England. Separate British consuls at Benin and Biafra

Time Chart

DATE	THE GAMBIA	SIERRA LEONE	GHANA	NIGERIA
1854	Civilian hospital opened. Cluny sisters became nurses			Courts of equity set up to help British consuls. S. A. Crowther became first Bishop on the Niger
			[*French began to extend rule inland in West Africa*	
1855	West Indian Mission to West Africa began work	Americans opened new mission at Shenge		
			[*Britain imported 50,000 tons of palm-oil from W.A.*	
1857				Factories set up at Aboh, Onitsha and Lokoja
1858		British show of force in Kambia		Ibadan at war with Ijebu and Oyo with Ijaye
1859				Ibadan and Dahomey allied with Oyo, Abeokuta, Ijebu, Ilesha and Ilorin with Ijaye
1860		Temne expelled missionaries from Magbele		
1861		British Governor 'acquired' Sherbro and British Koya		King Dosunmu of Lagos bribed by British to declare his town a British colony
1862				Pepple of Bonny now restored

West Africa in History

DATE	THE GAMBIA	SIERRA LEONE	GHANA	NIGERIA
1863		Executive and Legislative Councils elected	Asante defeated Br. West India regiment at Asikuma and Bobikuma	*President Lincoln of the U.S.A. freed all negro slaves there*
1865	Gambia once more governed from S.L.	S.L. alone not recommended by Select Committee for eventual self-government	G.C. once more governed from S.L.	Lagos governed from S.L. British consul sent to Lokoja
			[*Select Committee's Report on West African colonies*	
1866			Asante-Awuna alliance formed *v.* British—Ada, Ga, Akwapim. Aggrey deported.	
1867			Mankessim confederation formed. Kofi Karikari succeeded Kwaku Dua as Asantehene. Sweet River agreed by British and Dutch as dividing their spheres	
1868		Border clashes with Liberia		
1869	Cholera killed one quarter of population of Bathurst		Mankessim confederation of Fante kings at war with Elmina and Asante	British consul withdrawn from Lokoja
1870			[*Germany defeated France*	

148

Time Chart

DATE	THE GAMBIA	SIERRA LEONE	GHANA	NIGERIA
1871		Border clashes with Liberia	Fante kings met again at Mankessim	
1872			English acquired Elmina and other Dutch forts by purchase	
1873			Wolseley defeated Asante and took Kumasi	
1874			Treaties of Fomena and Dzelukofe. G.C. administration finally separated from S.L.	Lagos administered with G.C. instead of with S.L.
1875	Fula King Musa Molloh attacked Mandingo and Jola kings	Yoni attacked traders on Rokel	Mensa Bonsu Asantehene. Slavery and slave trade made illegal to all	Slavery and slave trade made illegal to all
1876	Soninke-Marabout wars ended; feud between Musa Molloh and Fodi Kabba opened	Fourah Bay College affiliated to Durham University		
1877		Mende King Bokari Gomna attacked Massaquoi of Sulima		
1879			Anglican Church founded in Accra. Tetteh Quashie introduced cocoa	

DATE	THE GAMBIA	SIERRA LEONE	GHANA	NIGERIA
1880				Goldie's Niger Co. dominated trade
			[European powers began 'Scramble for Africa']	
1881			R.C. Church founded at Elmina	Lagos-Abeokuta feud
1882		Scarcies and Moa accepted British protection		Thompson signed treaties with Sokoto and Gwandu
1883		Yoni attacked Fula traders at Rotifunk	End of Mensa Bonsu's reign as Asantehene	Carter signed treaties with Oyo, Ilorin, Abeokuta and Ibadan
			[French annexed Dahomey and entered Bamako]	
1884			Kwaku Dua II became Asantehene	Lugard signed treaties with Kaiama and Nikki
			[Germany declared protectorate over Cameroons, French reached Timbuktu]	
1885		Yoni attacked Loko at Songo		British protectorate established over Niger districts and entrusted by British Government to Niger Co.
			[French seized Haute-Volta and Niger; Germany Togoland and Cameroons]	
1886		S.L.-Liberia border agreed		

Time Chart

DATE	THE GAMBIA	SIERRA LEONE	GHANA	NIGERIA
1887		Yoni attacked Madame Yoko of Senehun. Makaia attacked Sulima		
1888	Gambia separated finally from S.L.	British joined Kittam kings to defeat Makaia	Kwaku Dua III (Prempeh) became Asantehene	
1889	Kansala treaties signed	Mandingo King Samori helped King of Kaliere to besiege Falaba		
1890	Anglo-French commission drew Gambia boundaries	Makaia deported to G.C.	Prempeh of Asante refused to sign treaty with British	
1891			80 lb. of cocoa exported	
1892	British defeated Fodi Kabba finally	Bai Bureh helped British to subdue other kings	Prempeh sent messenger to London to the Queen	
1893				Yoruba wars ended
		[Guinea and Ivory Coast seized by France		
1894	Protectorate formed			
1895	West India regiment finally withdrawn	Railway started. Boundaries agreed with French. Freetown Municipality created	British conquered Asante	

West Africa in History

DATE	THE GAMBIA	SIERRA LEONE	GHANA	NIGERIA
1896		Protectorate formally declared	Asantehene Prempeh exiled to S.L. and Seychelles	
1897			Sarbah founded Aborigines' Rights Protection Society	
1898		Protectorate rising against colony and foreigners	British, French and Germans agreed on G.C. boundaries	Northern Nigeria's boundaries agreed between Britain and France
			[French finally defeated Samori	
1899				Railway started
1900	Marabout of Sankandi killed members of British expedition		Railway started	British Nigeria proclaimed
1901	British took Medina, Fodi Kabba's headquarters		Railway reached Tarkwa. Asante declared a British colony and administered with G.C.	Lagos to Kano railway started
1902	Total public revenue £50,000		Legislative and Executive Councils set up, but almost entirely official	
1903		Death of Sir Samuel Lewis		

Time Chart

DATE	THE GAMBIA	SIERRA LEONE	GHANA	NIGERIA
1904	King Wappai of Foni fled before British troops		Railway reached Kumasi from Sekondi	
1905		British troops defended Fabunde of Luawa against Kafura		
1906	Slave Trade Abolition Ordinance passed in the Gambia	Daru became HQ of West African Frontier Force in S.L.		Lagos administered with S. Nigeria
			[Rubber first grown commercially in Liberia	
1908		Railway reached Pendembu		
1910			20,000 tons of cocoa being exported	
1912		Parts of Gola Forest given to Liberia in exchange for parts of Luawa		Tin discovered at Jos and coal at Enugu
1913				Kano and Lagos linked by rail
1914		Railway reached Makeni		Egba brought into Southern Protectorate. Nigerian administration unified
			[Outbreak of World War I	
1915	Gambian troops sent to Cameroons			Jebba Bridge opened

West Africa in History

DATE	THE GAMBIA	SIERRA LEONE	GHANA	NIGERIA
1917	Gambian troops sent to Tanganyika			
1918		Motorable roads built in colony outside Freetown		Egba rose against British, but crushed
1919			Part of Togoland administered with Gold Coast	Part of Cameroons administered with Nigeria. Lugard retired
			[Togoland and Cameroons each divided between Britain and France	
1920		Dr Bankole Bright and Mr F. W. Dove attended Accra meeting of National Congress of British W.A.	National Congress of British West Africa met in Accra	Eleko of Lagos joined Herbert Macaulay in opposing water-rate and was deported
1922				Legislative Council given its first elected members
1923			Railway reached Accra	Macaulay's National Democratic Party won Lagos elections
1924		Legislative Council given its first elected members	Prempeh returned to Kumasi	

Time Chart

DATE	THE GAMBIA	SIERRA LEONE	GHANA	NIGERIA
1925			First elected members admitted to Legislative Council	
			[Ladipo Solanke formed West African Students Union in Britain	
1926		Temporary Municipal Board created in Freetown	Provincial Councils of Kings now meeting	
			[Firestone Rubber Co. given large concession by Liberian Govt.	
1927			Native Administration Ordinance	Anti-tax riots in Warri and Kwale
1928		Road building in protectorate started. City Council restored in Freetown		N.D.P. won Lagos elections
1929				Women's rising in Owerri and Calabar, Aba and Opobo
1930	Abolition of Slavery Ordinance passed	Diamonds discovered in Kono		
1932				Makurdi Bridge opened. Present railway system completed
1933				N.D.P. again won the Lagos elections

West Africa in History

DATE	THE GAMBIA	SIERRA LEONE	GHANA	NIGERIA
1935	Executive and Legislative Councils still entirely nominated		Sir Osei Agyeman Prempeh II enstooled as Asantehene	
1936				Nigerian Youth Movement formed by Ernest Okoli, soon joined by Dr Nnamdi Azikiwe
1937				Search for oil begun by Shell D'Arcy
1939		New Executive and Legislative Councils still had official majorities		
			[Second World War broke out	
1940		Protectorate and colony road systems linked		
1941				Rift between Dr Azikiwe and Mr Okoli
1943				Alhaji Abubakar Tafawa Balewa and Mallam Aminu Kano formed Bauchi Improvement Association

Time Chart

DATE	THE GAMBIA	SIERRA LEONE	GHANA	NIGERIA
1944				Dr Azikiwe formed National Council of Nigeria and the Cameroons
1946	Bathurst Town Council elected majority	Protectorate Assembly and District Councils created	Legislative Council given non-official majority	
1947	Legislative Council given 2 elected members	Executive and Legislative Councils first given African majorities	George Grant, Dr Danquah, R. S. Blay and F. Awoonor Williams formed United G.C. Convention. Dr Kwame Nkrumah returned home	[R.D.A. Formed [French Union of The Fourth Republic Legislative Council enlarged in numbers and jurisdiction and given non-official majority
1948		Mayoralty restored in Freetown	Accra riots. Univ. College of Ghana founded	Regional Houses of Assembly and of Chiefs set up. Egba Omo Oduduwa formed
1949			Convention People's Party founded after rift between Dr Danquah and Dr Nkrumah	[I.O.M. Formed by Leopold Senghor Bauchi Improvement Association expanded to become Northern People's Congress under leadership of Sardauna of Sokoto, Sir Ahmadu Bello

DATE	THE GAMBIA	SIERRA LEONE	GHANA	NIGERIA
1950		Rural Area Council formed. The Sierra Leone People's Party formed by Dr M. A. S. Margai and Mr Lamina Sankoh	C.P.P. won municipal elections	
1951	Legislative Council given 8 unofficial members, and first ministers appointed	The S.L.P.P. won first nation-wide elections. Legislative Council reconstituted	C.P.P. won General Elections. 'Representative Members' appointed	House of Representatives and Council of Ministers created. Action Group formed
1952			Dr Nkrumah Leader of Government Business. Kumasi College of Technology founded	N.P.C. won General Elections in North, A.G. in West, N.C.N.C. in East
1953	Consultative Committee advised British Colonial Secretary on further constitutional reforms	Ministers appointed	Regional, district, urban, municipal and local councils instituted	Regional Assemblies enlarged and given legislative powers. Threatened North-South split
1954	Legislative Council given elected majority. Executive Council given Gambian majority	Dr M. A. S. Margai appointed Chief Minister	C.P.P. won General Elections	Lagos constitutional conference followed 1953 London one

Time Chart

DATE	THE GAMBIA	SIERRA LEONE	GHANA	NIGERIA
1955				N.C.N.C.–N.E.P.U. alliance won in West and East in federal General Elections
1956	Chiefs' Conference established in the Gambia	Legislative Council became House of Representatives	C.P.P. won General Elections	N.C.N.C.–N.P.C. govt. in federation; N.P.C. in North; N.C.N.C. in East; A.G. in West
1957		S.L.P.P. won General Elections	250,000 tons of cocoa exported. March 6th independence under Dr Nkrumah's leadership	Another London constitutional conference. East and West became self-governing
			[General Elections in French West Africa	
1958		Dr Margai became Prime Minister		Final constitutional conference. North became self-governing. Final General Elections
			[French colonies in Africa offered independence. French Community Formed	
1959				Alhaji (later Sir) Abubakar Tafawa Balewa became Federal Prime Minister

West Africa in History

DATE	THE GAMBIA	SIERRA LEONE	GHANA	NIGERIA
1960	Mr Pierre Njie became Chief Minister of the Gambia	Executive and Legislative Councils all-African. London constitutional conference		October 1st independence under leadership of Alhaji Sir Abubakar Tafawa Balewa
1961	[*French Community breaks up; French-speaking countries fully independent. Formation of Union Africaine et Malgache; Casablanca group; Monrovia group*	April 27th independence under leadership of Sir Milton Margai	University of Ghana and Kwame Nkrumah University of Science and Technology founded	University of Nigeria founded at Nsukka Feb. S. Cameroons join Fed. Republic of Cameroun; N. Cameroons join Fed. of Nigeria. Regional elections in Nigeria
1962	Mr (later Sir) Dawda Jawara became Premier of the Gambia		University College of Cape Coast founded First attempt on President Nkrumah's life.	Universities founded at Lagos, Ife and Zaria Political crises in Western Region. First census.
1963	Election challenged by Mr N'Jie declared valid by Privy Council	General Elections S.L.P.P. majority, Sir Milton Margai Prime Minister	Jan. Dr Danquah again detained. Progress of Volta River and Tema projects	Chiefs Awolowo and Enahoro sentenced. Mid-West Region created. October 1st Nigeria becomes a Republic. [*Jan. M. Sylvanus Olympio (Togo) assassinated. May. Organization of African Unity established at Addis Ababa*]

160

Time Chart

DATE	THE GAMBIA	SIERRA LEONE	GHANA	NIGERIA
1964	Failure of negotiations regarding integration between the Gambia and Senegal. July. Constitutional Conference in London	April. Death of Sir Milton Margai. Mr (Sir) Albert Margai succeeds him as P.M. Sept. Njala University opened	Jan. Ghana becomes a one-party state. President given power to dismiss judges	Feb. Second census results announced. Further political crisis in the West. Oil production rapidly increasing in East. Dec. Federal elections – boycott by U.P.G.A. [*U.A.M. dissolved – U.A.M. de Co-operation Economique formed*
1965	Feb. 18. The Gambia wins independence. Nov. Referendum on change to Republic. Necessary two-thirds majority not obtained		June. General elections. C.P.P. take all seats. President Nkrumah re-elected. April. Dr Danquah died in prison	Supplementary elections. Broad-based government formed under Alhaji Sir Abubakar Tafawa Balewa. Serious disorders in Western Nigeria during and after elections. [*O.A.U. meeting in Addis Ababa Rhodesia crisis*

DATE	THE GAMBIA	SIERRA LEONE	GHANA	NIGERIA
1966	March 9. Sir Dawda Jawara knighted by the Queen.		Feb. 24. Dr Nkrumah deposed. National Liberation Committee takes over government under Major-General J. A. Ankrah	Jan. 11–12. Commonwealth Prime Ministers' Conference at Lagos. Jan. 15 16. Army takes over power. Sir Ahmadu Bello, Chief S. L. Akintola, Sir Abubakar Tafawa Balewa killed. Constitution suspended

INDEX

Abeokuta, 37, 38, 39, 40, 41, 42, 44
Abora, Battle of, 23
Aborigines' Rights Protection Society, 64, 65
Accra, 24, 27, 29, 30, 33, 35, 45, 46, 63, 64, 65, 67, 69, 77, 79, 98, 101, 117, 118, 129
Afrique Occidentale Francaise (A.O.F.), 92
Akim (people), 24, 26, 27, 32
Akim Abuakwa, 24, 66
Akintola, S. L., 43, 83, 97, 120, 121, 123, 125, 126
Akitoye, King, 38, 39, 41, 42
Akwapim (people), 24, 27, 30
Alakija, Sir Adeyemo, 80
American Colonization Society, 103, 104, 105
Apam (fort), 24, 29, 30
Appiah, Joe, 97, 118
Armattoe, Dr Raphael, 97
Asante (people), 18, 23, 24, 26, 27, 29, 30, 31, 32, 33, 34, 48, 56, 57, 60, 63, 65, 66, 67, 70, 73, 137
Ashmun, Jehudi, 103, 104
Asikuma, Battle of, 29
Assin (people), 23, 27, 28, 31, 32
Awolowo, Obafemi, 80, 83, 87, 121, 125
Awuna (people), 30, 33
Azikiwe, Dr Nnamidi, 75, 77, 79, 80, 81, 83, 86, 87, 88, 97, 121, 123, 138

Badagry, 39, 41, 42
Balewa, Alhaji Sir Abubaka Tafawa, 80, 87, 88, 125, 126
Bathurst, 12, 13, 14, 15, 16, 20, 59, 112

Bello, Sir Ahmadu, 53, 120, 125, 126
Benin, 43, 44, 45, 46, 72, 74, 81, 87, 123
Beyin (fort), 24, 30
Bini (people), 42, 44, 45, 49, 74, 87
Bobikuma, Battle of, 29
Bokari Gomna, King, 21
Bond, The, 28, 29, 70, 137
Bonny, 45, 46, 47, 48, 49, 50, 51, 124
Bornu, 52, 53, 54, 55, 73
Brass, 44, 49, 51
Bullom, 18

Calabar, 35, 45, 46, 47, 49, 50, 51, 74, 75, 76, 78, 81, 87
Cameroun People's National Democratic Party, 127
Cape Coast, 20, 23, 24, 26, 28, 30, 64, 65, 69, 75, 117
Christian missions, 108, *See* Anglican, Methodist, Catholic, Church Missionary Society, Brethren in Christ
Christianity, 20
Christiansborg (fort), 26, 27, 29, 30, 67
Clifford Constitution, 75
cocoa, 33, 57, 58, 63, 67, 68, 108, 114, 116, 122, 131
Company of Merchants, 11, 13, 17, 24, 26
Convention People's Party, 69, 70, 117, 118, 119
Coussey Committee, 68
Creoles, 20, 21, 22, 62, 113

Dakar, 92, 93, 94, 95, 101, 102, 133
Dala Modu (Chief), 18
Danquah, Dr J. B., 67, 68, 117, 118
Deer Island, 15
Delta states, 49
Denkyera (People), 26, 27, 28, 31, 32
Diori, Hamani, 133
Dodowa, 26, 27
Dosunmu, 39

Edo (language), 43
Egba (people), 36, 37, 38, 39, 40, 41, 42, 71, 72, 74, 75
Eleduwe War, 40
Elmina, 24, 27, 29, 30, 31, 32, 33
Enahoro, Anthony, 83, 121
Endeley, Dr E. M. L., 127
Enugu, 81

Fante, 20, 23, 24, 26, 27, 28, 30, 31, 32, 64, 137
Firestone Company of America, 107, 109
Fodi Kabba, 16, 17, 57, 58
Foncha, John, 127
Fourah Bay College, 18, 20, 61
Freetown, 11, 12, 15, 17, 18, 19, 20, 21, 22, 23, 37, 61, 62, 113
French National Assembly, 90, 93, 95
Fula (people), 14, 15, 16, 17, 18, 21
Fulani, 35, 36, 37, 40, 49, 51, 52, 53, 54, 55, 56, 57, 73, 89, 137
Futa Jallon, 18

Ga (people), 24, 26
Gold Coast Aborigines' Rights Society, 34, 137
Guggisberg Constitution, 65

Hausa, 20, 52, 53, 54, 89, 133
Hill (governor), 19, 21, 27, 28, 61
Hlubi, Marko, 97
Houphouet-Boigny, Felix, 95, 96, 100, 130

Ibadan, 37, 38, 39, 40, 41, 42, 71, 79, 81, 86, 87, 91
Ibo, 18, 20, 46, 47, 48, 49, 50, 73, 74, 80, 83
Ife (people), 35, 36, 37, 40, 43, 87
Igbajo war, 40
Ijaiye, 38, 39, 40, 42
Ijebu (people), 36, 37, 40
Ilorin, 35, 36, 40, 53, 56, 72, 87
Indépendants d'Outre Mer' (I.O.M.), 95
Islam, 14, 15, 20, 35, 37, 52, 53, 54, 85, 91, 96, 134
Itsekiri (people), 44, 46, 49, 87

Jaja, King, 48, 49, 51
James Island, 12, 17
Jawara, David, 60, 111, 112
Johnson, Dr J. C. de Graft, 97
Johnson, I. T. A. Wallace, 62, 77, 97
Jola (people), 14, 16, 17
Joloff (people), 14, 91
Jukun (people), 52

Index

Kamerun National Democratic Party, 127
Kanemi, Sheikh Muhammed El Amin El, 53, 54, 55, 56
Kano, Aminu, 80, 85, 125
Keita, Modibo, 95, 96, 130, 131, 132, 134
Kenyatta, Dr Jomo, 97
Kofi, Karikari (Asantehene), 31, 32
Kollimanka Mane, 12
Kombo, 11, 12, 15, 59
Kommenda, 24, 29, 30
Kontagora, 56, 73
Kormantine, 23, 29, 30
Kosoko, 38, 39, 41, 42
Kumasi, 24, 26, 27, 31, 32, 33, 34, 63, 64, 67, 69, 91, 117
Kwadwo Otibu (Assin King), 23, 26
Kwaku Dua (Asantehene), 27, 30, 31, 33

Lagos, 16, 20, 30, 33, 36, 37, 38, 39, 40, 41, 42, 43, 44, 45, 51, 57, 72, 73, 74, 75, 76, 77, 78, 79, 81, 83, 84, 85, 86, 87, 100, 101, 118, 121, 122, 123, 125, 126, 137
Limba (people), 21, 22
Loko (people), 18, 21, 22
Loko, Port, 17, 18, 19, 22
Lugard, Lord, 66, 73, 74, 75, 138

MacCarthy (governor), 11, 12, 14, 16, 17, 18, 26
Macpherson Constitution, 81, 82
Maga, Hubert, 127
Makaia, 22

Mandingo (people), 14, 16, 21, 89, 91
Mankessim, 30, 31, 34, 137
Marabout (Muslim sect), 14, 15, 16, 17, 57
Margai, Sir Albert, 113
Margai, Sir Milton A. S., 62, 63, 113
Mende (people), 18, 19, 20, 21, 22
Mensa Bonsu, (Asantehene), 32
missionaries, 13, 14, 17, 18, 19, 21, 23, 29, 30, 31, 32, 38, 39, 40, 42, 45, 50, 55, 137
Mori (fort), 29, 30
Mossi (People), 91, 136
Musa Molloh (King), 16, 57
Muslims. *See* Islam

Nanna, 44, 45, 46
National Council of Nigeria and the Cameroons (N.C.N.C.), 43, 79, 80, 81, 83, 85, 88, 95, 120, 121, 125
Niger, river, 21, 35, 36, 44, 49, 50, 51, 55, 71, 72, 74, 91, 121, 124, 128, 133, 137
Nigerian Action Group, 80, 83, 85, 88, 120, 121, 123, 125
Nigerian National Alliance, 125
Nigerian National Democratic Party, 43, 75, 76, 77, 125
Nigerian Youth Movement, 43, 77, 79, 81
Nkrumah, Dr Kwame, 67, 69, 70, 77, 97, 99, 115, 116, 117, 118, 119, 138
Northern Elements' Progressive Union (N.E.P.U.), 80, 85, 125
Northern Peoples' Congress (N.P.C.), 80, 82, 83, 85, 88, 125

Nsamankow, battle of, 26

oil, 124, 131
oil palm, 21, 27, 35, 46, 47, 48, 50, 51, 58, 74, 106, 112, 114, 122
Okpara, Dr Michael, 120, 125
Oluyedun, Are Ona Kakanfo, 38
Oluyole, Basorun, 38
Olympio, Sylvanus, 96
Opobo, 48, 49, 50, 51, 76
Opubu, The Great, 46
Organization for African Unity (O.A.U.), 90, 101, 102, 116, 136
Osei Bonsu, (Asantehene), 23, 26
Osei Yaw Akoto (Asantehene), 26, 27
Overami, Oba, 45, 46
Owu war, 37
Oyo, 35, 36, 37, 38, 40, 41, 43, 44, 56, 74

Sagrenti. *See* Wolseley, Sir Garnet
Saint Mary's Island, 11, 12, 13, 17
Samori (King), 21, 57, 63
Sarbah, J. Mensah, 34, 64
Scarcies, 20, 21
Sekondi (fort), 24, 29, 30
Senghor, Leopold, 94, 95, 96, 99, 111, 134
Sherbro, 18, 19, 20, 21, 23, 62, 103
Sierra Leone People's Party, 62, 63, 95, 113
slave trade, 11, 12, 17, 18, 24, 27, 28, 35, 36, 41, 45, 46, 49, 50, 51, 92, 104, 106, 137
Sodeke, 37, 38
Soglo, Christopher, 128
Soninke (Muslim sect), 15, 16, 17, 57
steamships, 5, 15, 48, 51
Susu (People), 17, 18, 89

Pan African Congress, 97, 98
Parti Dahoméan de l'Unité, 127
Parti Démocratique de la Côte d'Ivoire, 94, 95, 130
Pepple,William Dappa, 46, 47, 48
Prempeh (Asantehene), 33, 66

Temne (People), 17, 18, 19, 21, 22
Tinubu, Madame, 39, 42
Touré, Sékou, 96, 98, 99, 129, 130
Tubman, President, 99, 107, 108, 109

railways, 22, 61, 63, 71, 74, 86, 117, 121
Rassemblement Démocratique Africain (R.D.A.), 94, 95, 98, 127, 130, 131
Richards Constitution, 78, 81
Roberts, Joseph Jenkins, 105, 106
Royal Niger Company, 71, 72, 73

Umoru, Nagwamatse, 56
Union Africaine et Malgache (U.A.M.), 99, 100, 102, 128, 130, 133, 136
Union Démocratique Dahoméene, 127
United Africa Company, 51
United Gold Coast Convention, 67

Index

United Nations, 88, 97, 107, 111, 120, 122, 127
United Progressive Grand Alliance (U.P.G.A.), 125
Usman, Dan Fodio, 51, 52, 53, 54, 56

Volta River Project, 115, 139

Wassaw (People), 31
Watson Commission, 68, 80
Willink Commission, 87, 88
Wolseley, Sir Garnet, 32, 33
World War I (1914-18), 58, 61, 74, 75, 94, 106, 107

World War II (1939-45), 58, 59, 61, 64, 75, 77, 78, 94, 95, 97, 109, 138
Wuli, 15

Yaa Asantewa, 34
Yalunka (people), 18
Yameogo, President, 118, 136
Yoko (Madame), 21
Yoni (people), 21, 23
Yoruba, 20, 35, 36, 38, 43, 53, 56, 71, 72, 137
Yoruba (people), 18, 35, 36, 37, 41, 50, 74, 80, 83, 87

Zikist Movement, 81

Printed in Great Britain
by Amazon